On Behalf of the Wolf
and the First Peoples

NICHOLAS PIEROTTI

On Behalf
of the Wolf
and the
First Peoples

Joseph Marshall III

For Yuri

and

For Mahpiyata Waci

and

For their mothers.

FIRST EDITION

Manufactured in the United States of America
Cover painting by Eugene Ridgely Jr.
Cover and Text design by Dana Herkelrath
Interior Illustrations by Devon and Dana Herkelrath

Library of Congress Cataloging-in-Publication Data

Marshall, Joe.
    On behalf of the wolf and the first peoples:essays / Joseph Marshall III ; foreword by Roger Welsch—1st ed.
        p.   cm.
    ISBN 1-878610-45-7
    1. Indian philosophy — North America. 2. Indians, Treatment of — North America. 3. Indians of North America—Social life and customs. I. Title.
E98 . P5M35   1995
973' . 0497—dc 20
                                                    95-41844
                                                    CIP

Permission given by the University of Nebraska Press to quote from *The Ponca Chiefs*, by Thomas Henry Tibbles, copyright 1971

Red Crane Books
2008 Rosina Street
Suite B
Santa Fe, New Mexico   87505

Contents

Foreword

Whites stole the land—gardens, burial sites, holy places, and all—from the Indian. Sometimes they even took the names with the land—Nebraska, Kansas, Dakota. They lifted a few ideas like the moccasin or canoe, thus backhandedly acknowledging certain Native American technological superiorities and grudgingly, sometimes, tried Indian foods, rejecting them, however, once famine had passed. After all, what would the neighbors think if they came visiting and found you eating…*Indian* food!

I can't help but imagine, knowing something about Native American customs of the past and present and quite a bit about human nature, that Indians all across the continent, wherever the plague of the frontier touched, must have wondered why more such "borrowing" didn't go on. Why do these pale people eat stinking, maggoty pork hanging half-frozen in a barn, when the advantages of dried and smoked buffalo or beef or venison should be fairly obvious? Why do they continue to grow their puny vegetables that struggle so to survive every year when the wild plants that provided an abundant larder for the Indians were systematically ignored—tipsin, milkweed, artichokes, groundnuts? Throughout history, after all, tribe had always borrowed and learned from tribe; how else could corn, tobacco, coyote stories, pottery, knowledge of the Powers spread from people to people?

So why do the pale people freeze in their thin-walled frame houses when the advantages of the earth-lodge and tipi are so evident? Why do they struggle with fragile narrow wheels in soft sands and over torturous rocks when a pony drag is so comfortable and mobile? Why kill Mother Earth when she is so generous with her bounty?

I have written elsewhere that as if those questions were not puzzling enough, as if the white man's thievery were not widespread enough, the riddle is even greater: why did the invaders steal so little? And when they did steal so much, why did they take only the least valuable of the treasures? What of the riches of the mind and spirit that were left untouched?

Many angry Native Americans—angry not at me and my questions but at history and its injustices—have made it clear that they do not share that assessment. The white man, they say, as if he had not stolen enough already, now has his eye on the very relationships between Indians and their gods. Now they want to steal his soul. The white man's stink profanes the sweat lodge and robs it of its purity; white Catholic priests inflict their blasphemous presence on the powerful rituals of the sun dance; white anthropology professors dare to sit at the Blackfoot drum and sing the old songs—badly; "Navajo" baskets with tabu symbols—made in Taiwan! — are sold by white traders; white Boy Scouts affect traditional Omaha costume and imitate dances that have always been, and always will be, Omaha; a white suburban housing development is called Wakonda Heights— "God Heights!" Perhaps one white man can say too little has been stolen, but for many Native Americans it has been quite enough, thank you.

A part of the disagreement, of the mis-understanding, arises from the fact that there is a hierarchy of cultural materials that must be understood before cultural exchanges can be understood, and that hierarchy is all too often ignored by whites and Indians, scholars and laymen alike. First, most basically, there is a level of *item*, the thing, the object. Whether that item is a song, a way of greeting a friend, the nature of wealth, or an actual object like a moccasin, it is simply a thing. A lot of older, smaller museums are item oriented: there are cases of things—a World War I rifle, a box of arrowheads found on a farm not far from the museum, the remains of a two-headed calf, a spinning wheel brought to this state on a covered wagon. They rest in their glass cases or hang on the wall with the intention of surprising or amusing or startling the viewer, but no information of value or interest passes into the eye and mind of the museum guest.

When objects have been accepted, adopted, or stolen by white culture from Indian culture, it has usually been at the level of "item." Maize seeds are taken from Indian gardens and grown in the gardens of a white family. It's as simple (and uninteresting) as that.

The next level of culture is *context*, the matrix within which an item exists historically, culturally, geographically, religiously, that sort of thing. Museums have tried to accommodate this facet of the complexities of culture by developing "period rooms," exhibits where the spinning wheel is shown as an item of furniture in a pioneer home or as a part of the entire inventory of a Conestoga wagon. Maps trace the development of corn as it moved across space and time within the Native American world, or how it functions now within American, or worldwide mainstream culture. A diorama of a Pawnee village shows a field of corn as it was cultivated before the arrival of the frontier on the Plains.

Contexts certainly add to our understanding of items, but there is still a lot missing. How does the spinning wheel work By what process did the Indians grow corn? How did the Pilgrims grow corn? How was it prepared to be eaten then, and how is it now converted to energy or fed to animals to be eaten later?

Now we are approaching the level of process, and museums have responded to that dynamic by developing "living history" programs, where visitors can see, hear, smell, taste, feel all of the impulses that process provides. What's curious at this point is that the basic principles of the item-oriented examination are now no longer important: in an item-oriented museum what is important is the item—that it is authentic, that it is the real thing, that this is indeed the spinning wheel brought to this county in a covered wagon. As we examine process, we don't need the old spinning wheel. In fact, it may be too fragile for us to touch, yet alone put to work again. We may be using an accurate replica of a nineteenth-century spinning wheel in our demonstrations. It doesn't matter. The sounds, smells, feels, tastes, and final products—sweat, blistered fingers, clogged lungs, and a wisp of thread—are the same, and that's what counts.

The next stage in study and interpretation is meaning. It is at this level that the most learning takes place, and the most work; and the most excitement, and the most and greatest demands on the intellect and spirit. And yet there really cannot be understanding without at least consideration being turned to meaning. Those of us who are not Navajo can never understand a Navajo coyote story until we grasp not only the item of the story itself, the context in which it is told historically and culturally, the manner in which it is told, and its meaning—why it can be told only at certain times of the year, what Coyote and his ways and his stories mean to the people themselves. If then. It's entirely possible; of course, that those of us who are not Navajo will never understand a coyote story because we cannot. Because we are not Navajo.

It is one thing to see the spinning wheel, another to know where and when it lived, what its working was like...it is another to understand what that tool meant—a sense of independence for a family that it could manufacture its own clothing, a sense of despair that a woman was so chained to her spinning wheel that nearly omnipotent witches like Circe or rich and powerful princesses in fairytales are still women and so must still be locked eternally to the damnable wheel. And why is that wheel not worn out in the item-oriented museum? Because there were no fibers to be spun once the frontier reached the Plains and no need for the labor because cloth was readily purchasable from the local general store. Or easily ordered from Sears and Roebuck. Once we consider context, process, and meaning, the physical reality of an item becomes the least impressive element of its nature.

Now comes my friend Joseph Marshall III with his cultural gift for us, and I step back, confused by its complexity. Not by Joe Marshall's writing itself. That is straightforward enough: He takes his readers through a variety of items of Native American history and culture, providing us with context and process and, insofar as possible, meaning. *On Behalf of the Wolf and the First Peoples* is important, well written, and long overdue. It should be in every library and on the shelves of everyone who has an interest in Native American culture.

Native Americans have complained about non-Indians writing about Native American culture, and the inevitable, reasonable response has been, "Anyone can write a book about anything: what we need is more books, not fewer, and what we need most of all is more books about Native American culture by Native Americans." Okay, here it is. And Joe Marshall has done a dandy job, as I'm sure you'll agree, since the book is at this moment in your hands. At last we have a view of Native American culture from a Native American perspective.

To that degree *On Behalf of the Wolf and the First Peoples* doesn't need a lot of introduction. I am surprised not by what is in the book but that there is a book. What baffles me and convinces me all the more that the white man still hasn't stolen enough is not the content of this book, the substance of Joseph Marshall's gift, the item in question. The curiosity of Joseph Marshall's book is its position within the other three levels of the cultural paradigm: what has moved this traditionially-oriented Lakota, this doggedly insistent Native American, this studiedly Indian advocate to share today what he knows and feels—the process of the matter—with those of us who are not Native American—the context? Shouldn't he as an individual and as a Native American resent his context so bitterly that the very notion of sharing the most intimate, most profound, most cherished parts of his traditions with, of all people, us, repulse him? Shouldn't he punish us by withholding what he knows and feels?

Joseph Marshall's generosity is not new to me or others who spent time with Native Americans. As a stranger, having never so much as shaken hands with an Indian in so far as I know, thirty years ago I was welcomed into Omaha tribal gatherings, given a place of honor, and fed the best of what there was to eat. Committing cultural gaffe after cultural gaffe, I have nonetheless been embraced and included, not simply tolerated but... my god! ...*adopted.*

And yet for as often as I have received it, I have never become accustomed to Native American generosity and goodwill. I have never been less puzzled than I am at each new encounter. In fact, the more I have come to appreciate the power and persistence of Native American culture, the more I have wondered why those who are entitled to it would ever share it with those who come from a culture that has shown it so little regard. It is not for the white man to ask why the Native American has not been more generous, of course; the question can only be the opposite: why is the white man still welcome where he is? And here I am again: why, given all the great Native American voices of the past and present, has Joseph Marshall III invited me, a white man, to participate in this, his grand gift? I can only be grateful; I'll probably never be Indian enough to understand.

In short, even if we manage to grasp in a limited way the "item" of Joe Marshall's gift to us in this book, can we ever grasp the nature of its "context"—Joe Marshall's position as an Indian in the white man's world—or its "process"—his generosity?

As for the meaning of Joe Marshall's gift...well, he can't give us everything. Some things we just may need to figure out for ourselves. Perhaps for the moment, just as even today a Lakota vision or a moment of enlightenment in a Native American church prayer meeting is accepted without question (even though there may not be much more to it than question!), we will have to accept Marshall's generosity without fully understanding it, a glimpse of truth without explanation. Like recipients of a vision, as those of us not graced with Lakota blood read *On Behalf of the Wolf and the First Peoples*, we need to understand that what's important is not the gift but the giving, and we are fortunate to be offered the gift, truly blessed if we accept it.

— *Roger Welsch*

Acknowledgments

In a sense this project began when I was a boy listening to conversations between and stories told by many Lakota old people, especially my maternal and paternal grandparents. Although all of them have gone on to the next world, they will always be dear to my heart and will forever live in my memories. To the following my gratitude is undying: Albert Two Hawk, Annie Good Voice Eagle Two Hawk, Reverend Charles J. Marshall, Blanche Roubideaux Marshall, Katie Roubideaux Blue Thunder, Isaac Bear, Isaac Knife, Richard Mouse, Harris Lodgeskin Menard, Sam Brings Three White Horses, Moses Rattling Leaf, Lucy Little Bird Rattling Leaf, Maggie Little Bird Little Dog, Paul Little Dog, George Brave Boy, James Provincial, Olive Provincial, Lulu Lodgeskin, Millie Menard, and Wilson and Alice Janis. *Mitakuyepi, wopila tanka heca yelo.*

I owe a debt of gratitude also to my parents, Joseph Marshall II and Hazel Two Hawk Marshall, for many things, but most especially for bringing me into this world as a Lakota.

Several of these essays are adapted from columns that first appeared in the Casper Star-Tribune (Casper, Wyoming). Thank you to Robin Hurliss, Publisher, Annie McKinnon, Managing Editor, and especially to Claudette Ortiz, Letters Editor, for putting my words in front of the good people of Wyoming.

A special thanks to Mary Lou Morrison for recommending that I approach the Casper Star-Tribune with the first of my essays and for her friendship and support.

For encouragement, constructive critique, professionalism, but most of all for their humanity, a very special thanks to my editor Ann Mason of Santa Fe and Carol Caruthers, my editor at Red Crane Books.

To my friend Roger Welsch of Dannebrog, Nebraska, thank you for honoring this work with your wisdom and insight. I look forward to your next book.

Thank you to Eugene Ridgely Jr., Northern Arapaho, from the Wind River Reservation in Wyoming for the effort and talent imparted to the fine watercolor which became the cover of this book.

Thank you to my children: Kira, Michael, William, Erin, Steven, Caitlin, and one other, not only for being a source of inspiration, but also for embodying all of the outstanding attributes of Lakota children and young people and thus being part of the hope for the future of all Lakota people.

A very special appreciation to my mother-in-law, Carol B. Wilson, for her support and encouragement.

An equally special thanks to my friend and agent, Connie K. West.

Acknowledgments

My sincerest thanks to my wife, Sharon, without whom this book would not have been possible.

Finally, my profound appreciation to Marianne and Michael O'Shaughnessy, Editor and Publisher of Red Crane Books of Santa Fe, New Mexico. Thank you for enabling a Lakota boy from the res to speak his mind. *Mitakuye oyasin.*

Joseph Marshall III

On Behalf of the Wolf and the First Peoples

He came out of the the dark line of trees and walked to the cool mountain stream, standing for a moment in a small eddy, cooling his feet. He was big, gray, and old, but still powerful. A breeze ruffled his gray coat. He was magnificent.

Coming out of the water he walked slowly to a mossy bed on the stream bank. Fatigue showed in each slow, careful step. He lay down with his forepaws in the water and looked in my direction with old eyes that had seen much. The wisdom in them was easy to see. A slight smile of reassurance passed through them. He had sensed my fear.

He lifted a foot out of the water and methodically licked the pads. Now the other forefoot. That done, he looked at me and spoke. "Grandson, I have walked far," he said softly. "And my feet are tired." There was kindness and strength in that old voice. "But I am close to my journey's end. And I am glad."

I gathered courage to speak, not certain if I should dare lift my voice to this magnificent, old warrior. "Grandfather," I finally said. "Who are you? Where do you go?"

I saw a smile in his eyes again. "My name does not matter. What matters is that I am here, now. That we have this time together is why I have come, because we all share this journey: four-leggeds, two-leggeds, and those-who-fly. We are all related. And where I go, you may go also. Take heed."

The old warrior sighed. With narrowed eyes he tested the wind. Then he leaned forward and drank from the cold current. Sitting back, he stared off into the forest, but into some other place as well. His eyes reflected everything he saw. Suddenly, tipping back his head, he began to sing. Sharp and rhythmic barks at first. Then a long, high wail that died away softly. He sang again and again.

After he stopped I said, "Grandfather, that is a sad song."

He stood. "Yes. It is the song of my people. It is the song of my life. The song of my death." He looked off again into the far line of trees.

"You will leave?" I asked.

"Yes," he said. "My journey is almost over. I am glad or that. I am weary."

Walking into the stream, he stopped to cool his feet a last time. Crossing to the far bank, he turned to look into my eyes. Into my heart. "Grandson," he said. "I must ask something of you."

I waited.

"Sing my song," he pleaded with a tired voice. "Sing the song of my people. For I am afraid...." His voice trailed off. "I can give you nothing in return. Only that I will be with you in spirit."

I could not refuse. I nodded. "I will, Grandfather. I will sing your song."

"Good," he said. "You will come to know the ways and powers of my people as your own. Sing my song. Sing it well."

He looked long into my eyes. In his there was sadness, wisdom, kindness, and strength. But courage most of all. He turned. Without a sound he went into the forest and was gone.

On Behalf of the Wolf and the First Peoples

This dream first came to me when I was six years old. Being a child, I took the wolf's request literally and went around howling. My grandfather, I recall, seemed particularly interested in this sudden aberrant behavior. Since I was generally a quiet, unobtrusive child, my outbursts of wolf song piqued his curiosity. My grandmother, on the other hand, seemed to take it more in stride. Only once did she gently tell me that howling just outside the window at dusk, especially with a houseful of guests inside, was not a polite thing to do. I do recall now that one of the guests, an Episcopalian priest, did look at me as if seriously considering an exorcism. But he was a white man, and in his world the wolf was an evil thing. Since that moment I have met many like him. And I have learned more about the wolf.

Later that year came a reminder of the dream. It was on a crisp, late autumn evening as I was chasing my seventh year. I thought I heard a real wolf's howl. I had gone a few hundred yards to a bluff over the Little White River. I sat there feeling particularly connected to everything around me. The moon had just risen full and round. Its cool, orange presence touched the wolf in me, and I lifted my face and howled, trying to imitate exactly the wolf in my dream.

The air was cool, and sound carried great distances. Somewhere along the river bottom, inside the mostly leafless stands of oak, ash, and willow, a white-tailed buck snorted and stamped his feet. I had apparently convinced him that I was an elusive, shadowy, four-legged hunter on the prowl. Then, from a high ridge on the opposite side of the valley came a howl precisely like the one in my dream—a powerful voice singing a hauntingly sad and beautiful song, rising to a piercing crescendo and then falling away. The white-tailed buck snorted again, probably certain he was surrounded by a pack of wolves. Then the valley fell silent, except for the sounds of deer running on the leaf-covered valley floor. There was an air of expectancy. I waited, but there was no more singing.

After a long, lonely silence, I ran home to tell my grandparents that I had heard a wolf howl.

My grandmother smiled and looked at my grandfather. He quietly told me that there were no more wolves here and suggested that what I had heard was a coyote. There were coyotes around, and I *knew* a coyote's howl. What I had heard from across the valley was not a coyote. "I heard a wolf!" I insisted.

"How do you know?" my grandfather patiently asked.

"From the one in my dream," I replied.

My grandfather did not take dreams lightly. He coaxed me into revealing the one I had had about the wolf. After I finished, he reminded me that the last wolf in our part of the reservation had been hunted down and killed in 1917, thirty-four years before I had heard one howl from across the river. Then he said, "The wolf does not only want you to howl, he wants you to tell what happened to his people. That is what he meant when he asked you to sing his song. He wants you to learn about his people and tell others what happened to them."

"Why?" I wondered. "What happened to them?"

"Many of them were killed," my grandfather

said. "Very many. They were driven from their home … just like we were. We Lakota, and other people like us."

It was then that I began to learn that the wolf and I are brothers. That I am more like him than I ever imagined. Born into the same land of the same Mother. We are kindred spirits and fellow travelers in a common existence, bound together by respect, adversity, and challenge.

The dream has come several times over the years since my boyhood on the Rosebud Sioux Indian Reservation. It seems to come as a reminder at those times in my life when the frenetic, directionless pull of the non-Indian world threatens to tear another piece of my Lakota identity from me. It comes and comforts me, reassures me, and reminds me of the promise that I made to that old wolf.

The dream never changes. It plays in my memory like a movie rerun. And now and then I learn something new from it, and about it. Rather like noticing some new detail about a movie after seeing it for the twelfth time, such as, life is an individual and a common journey; or the fate of one kind of being is always connected somehow, somewhere, to the fate of all others; or that wisdom can exist even when it is communicated in an unknown language—in other words, humankind does not have a monopoly on wisdom.

Such new insights occur when I have reached a new level of maturity. To put it another way, the dream continually provides new and deeper insights, but only when I have earned the right to gain those new insights or have grown to a higher level of awareness. In a convoluted way the dream also provides the

Joseph Marshall III

incentive to earn the right to new insights, for example, by pushing me to learn many lessons about the wolf.

The first and most enduring lesson I have learned is regarding my kinship with the wolf—and, in a broader sense, the kinship between the first peoples of this continent and the wolf. This kinship took us down the same road and nearly to the same end. Even now we have much in common; and the paths we walk, if not joined, are certainly parallel.

The kinship of the wolf and the first peoples on Turtle Island (now called North America) is ancient. It was formed generations and millenniums ago and long, long before the two-leggeds learned arrogance. At that time people understood that they shared the land and their existence with other species and that two-leggeds were only a small part of the natural order.

The people of that time learned the ways of the wolf because they understood the reality of their existence. Among them it was the *hunter* and *warrior* who followed most closely the path of the wolf. As a hunter the wolf had no equal—with his keen eyesight, unimaginably sharp sense of smell, sharp teeth, and powerful jaws. Those were formidable weapons, but the first people saw that they were of little use without endurance, patience, and perseverance. These were even more important weapons of the wolf, and they were qualities the first peoples could develop in themselves. Also the first peoples saw the wolf as a warrior because he defended his family and his home regardless of the strength of the enemy or the odds he had to face. This was another lesson learned from the wolf.

On Behalf of the Wolf and the First Peoples

However, there was an even more profound lesson they learned from the wolf. Instead of fearing or envying the wolf, the first people knew they could emulate him. But to be like the wolf meant that *they* also had to exist to serve the environment—to accept the mutuality of life. This meant that they could take and use what they needed in order to live, so long as they understood that they could be used in the same way. Understanding this reality made them truly *of* the earth, because *every life* ultimately gives itself back to the earth. My grandfather and a dead deer showed me this essential truth.

During one of our long walks in the valley of the Little White River, my grandfather and I came upon a decomposing deer carcass. It did not smell particularly good, and it was being picked over by several turkey buzzards. There were signs of earlier feasting by other scavengers as well. Though I said nothing, my grandfather sensed my averse reaction to the sight.

"That deer has completed the circle," he told me. "He was born, he lived by taking from the land what he needed. When he died, his spirit left, perhaps to go back where it came from. Now his body is doing the same. In doing that, he is giving back the only thing that was truly his own—himself. The coyotes have been here, as the buzzards are now. By taking from him, they are helping him give. The same will happen to them some day. As it will happen to you and me. That's the way things are."

The wolf and the first peoples did not avoid the reality and the truths of their existence. They moved with the flow of life, not against it. Hunting

Joseph Marshall III

peoples, for example, did not put their villages in places that would disrupt the migratory patterns of game animals such as elk, bison, or caribou. No one erected a camp or built a village in a known floodplain. They understood the natural parameters bordering that existence and moved easily within them, comfortable with the places they had. Such commonsense thinking is apparently lost on our modern society, which builds towns, cities, roads, and bridges in areas prone to flooding or earthquakes or tornadoes or mudslides. Then when the floods do come or the earth moves or the twisters whirl, destroying homes, businesses, and lives, there is always ranting and raving about the "cruelty of nature." Perhaps there should be ranting and raving about the ignorance of man.

The first peoples understood that while they could emulate the wolf and be like wolf in some or many ways, they would never actually occupy the place wolf had. Furthermore, they understood that they had a power to understand and that this capacity set them apart from other species. Likewise, they knew that other species had at least one ability or characteristic that set each of them apart from other species, enhancing their chances of survival. The deer had keen senses of smell and hearing, the skunk had his scent, the porcupine had quills, the rattlesnake had poison, the owl could fly noiselessly, the bear had size and strength, the antelope had speed, and so on. In other words, the first peoples did not see their ability to reason or understand as anything that made them superior; instead, it was simply *their* key to survival.

On Behalf of the Wolf and the First Peoples

The first peoples not only survived, they thrived. They thrived because they did not seek to dominate. They understood that coexistence was the means to survival for all species because it was central to the reality of the shared physical world. No one species was dominant in all ways all of the time. The wolf certainly was not successful every time he went after prey. Neither was the human hunter. The bison's size, strength, and speed were not always enough to protect him every time a hunter approached. Observing these realities, the first peoples realized that it was best to let each species have its place and fulfill its contribution to the harmony of life. They perceived that dominance was not a natural part of the reality of the shared physical world. To attempt to dominate other species would be the same as moving against the flow and not with it. So the first peoples, like the wolf, took their places and never overstepped them. They learned to dance in step, in unison, with everything around them.

Unfortunately, those realities and those lessons from our past are lost upon us in the here and now. Coexistence is not a viable aspect nor an applied practice of today's dollar-driven technocratic society. Dominance of the human species over all others, in attitude and practice, is the norm. Dominance within the human species in the political, military, economic, racial (or ethnic), industrial, technological, and religious arenas of interaction is apparently the only philosophy that matters.

Of all the species of life on Turtle Island, the two that probably spread themselves the farthest over it

Joseph Marshall III

were the first peoples and the wolf. After thousands of years and hundreds and hundreds of generations of moving across the land, separate tribal identities began to emerge among the first peoples. Languages multiplied and customs developed. Lifestyles were influenced by geography, terrain, climate, and available resources. Some tribes remained nomads, while others became more sedentary. Some became farmers or fishermen while others continued to be gatherers. Still others remained primarily hunters.

The wolf, meanwhile, adapted himself to life in every kind of environment this continent had to offer. He was at home in the frozen tundras of the Arctic regions, the boiling deserts of the Southwest, the mountains, the forests, and the Great Plains. Furthermore, he existed virtually side by side with the first peoples. And he was referred to with as many labels or names as there were languages.

One Lakota word (or phrase) for wolf is *sungmanitu tanka*, generally meaning "big or great dog of the wilderness." But it is a recent label. The operative words are *sunka*, meaning dog, *manitu*, meaning wilderness, and *tanka* meaning big or great. *Sungmanitu tanka* is recent because the European or Euro-American concept of "wilderness" is used in the translation. Previous to European contact, the Lakota did not separate or compartmentalize, semantically or conceptually, the environment within which they lived and moved based on a narrow, exclusively anthropocentric sense of their place in it. There was no operative concept that the area in which they did not live was somehow "wild" or "wilder" than where they did live. To look at it another way, civilization was a concept and not a place. Therefore, the correct translation of *manitu* is simply "away from where humans are." *Sunkamanitu* or *sungmanitu* means "dog who lives apart from humans," or the coyote. *Sungmanitu tanka* is the "big or great dog who lives away from humans," the wolf. *Sunka* means simply "dog," the one who lives with humans. In today's vernacular, we would assume that the dog who lives with humans is or was "domesticated." But the first peoples of Turtle Island, Lakota or other tribes, did not think that the dog was "domesticated" any more than they perceived that the coyote and wolf lived in the "wild" or "wilderness." My grandfather was very insistent that I understood these distinctions.

Another Lakota word for wolf, probably older than any other, is *mayaca*. Although I am a Lakota speaker, I am not aware of its precise origins (though other Lakota speakers may be). My guess as to the origin of *mayaca* is that it denotes one who lives in a bank or a cliff face or some similiar terrain, since maya means either a steep riverbank (in a flowing or dry river) or a cliff face. Wolves are known to make dens in such terrain. In any case, it is only a guess, and in his stories my grandfather always used the more recent expression *sungmanitu tanka*.

Wolves and hunter-warriors, especially Lakota hunter-warriors, were the stuff of dreams for me as I grew up. Because my grandfather was a skillful storyteller, he created vivid images in my mind.

The earliest story of a wolf that I can recall is of the Dakota (as opposed to Nakota or Lakota) hunter who had waited in ambush and shot a buffalo with several arrows. Of course, the buffalo did not immediately die, so the hunter had to follow the wounded animal. The buffalo finally collapsed, and as the hunter hid and waited a safe distance to make sure the animal had expired, a wolf appeared and warily approached the buffalo. Displaying the utmost patience and caution, the wolf moved only a step at a time. Finally, she reached the downed buffalo, which by then had died. The wolf's demeanor and posture told the hidden hunter that the buffalo was dead and, therefore, it was safe to approach. But out of curiosity he waited to see what the wolf would do, fully expecting her to begin tearing at the flesh with her fangs. Instead, she went around and around the carcass until she saw the arrows protruding from the buffalo's side. She sniffed the arrows and then sat back on her haunches to carefully test the wind. After a time she looked directly toward the hunter's hiding place with a long, penetrating stare, and then nonchalantly walked away from the dead buffalo and disappeared over a rise. Later, after his wife and family had butchered the buffalo, the hunter made sure that they left behind some choice portions to share with the wolf and her family.

My favorite wolf story is about a young woman who lived with a family of wolves over a winter until the following spring. Of course, in my grandfather's story, the woman is Lakota. But since my boyhood I have heard similar stories from other tribes, and all of them have an almost identical story line. As the story goes, a woman leaves her home and village in heartbreak and

On Behalf of the Wolf and the First Peoples

anger because her husband has brought home a second, younger wife. It is late autumn, and she travels toward the village of some of her relatives. She becomes lost, her food supply is gone, and she faces the prospect of having to totally fend for herself or die of starvation. Eventually, she is found by a family of wolves, which leads her to shelter and occasionally brings her fresh meat. Over the winter she learns the nuances of their communication—their barks and howls—and is able to understand them. In the spring, they tell her that some of her people are moving close. After that, she leaves her wolf family and finally reaches the village of her relatives, who had received word that she was probably dead. Her relatives are overjoyed to see her and soon after give her the name Woman Who Lived with the Wolves.

Even today I can hear my grandfather's voice and see the hunter who shared his meat with a wolf, as well as Woman Who Lived with the Wolves as she sits outside her lodge, hears the wolves howling in the distance, and understands what they are saying. I can see a family of wolves sprinting across the prairie as they close in on a white-tailed deer, or playfully romping along a river, lazily dozing in the sun, or teaching their young how to stalk. Likewise, I can see mounted Lakota warriors riding through the dust at the Battle of the Greasy Grass (Little Bighorn) River or a spotted horse at a flying gallop as the hunter on its back draws his powerful sinew-backed flatbow and sends his arrow hissing into the side of a careening buffalo.

As powerful as these images were to me, and still are, there came a moment during my youth when

Joseph Marshall III

they were not enough. I wanted to see a real wolf and hear a real wolf song. I wanted a real Lakota warrior to come riding over the hill, lance in hand, bow and arrows slung across his back, the eagle feathers in his long black hair fluttering in the wind. But they were no more. Somewhere between the age of ten and twelve I had to reconcile with the fact that there were no wolves and no warriors in my world.

My grandfather said that he had heard that there were still wolves very far to the north, in Grandmother's Land—Canada. He hoped that I would travel there one day and see them. He held out no hope in seeing a Lakota warrior. "They have all died. There are no more warriors," he said. "There will never be again. Not like in the old times."

That night, with the covers over my head, I wept. I mourned for the wolves and the warriors that were gone from my world. I wept because there was nothing I could do to change that reality. But I think I also wept for an undefined loneliness, a longing for a part of my being and my heritage that had been taken from me, rather like how a cloud covering the sun quietly takes one's shadow.

After that night I vowed to myself that I would learn all I could about wolves and warriors—my rationale being that the more I knew about them, the more I could be like them. It was, I decided, the best way for me to bring them back. It was the only way for me to sing the song of the wolf.

During that learning process I subsequently discovered that the hunter-warriors of some tribes formed exclusive societies in which the wolf was the guiding spirit. Members of such societies emulated the wolf in the hunt, in battle, and sometimes in the way they dressed. Scout warriors who ventured into unknown or enemy territory as the eyes and ears for their people were often called "wolves." Many Plains hunters who hunted the buffalo often crawled on hands and knees, singly or in pairs, to the very edge of a herd, many times covered with wolf capes, and mimicking the movements and mannerisms of wolves. Since buffalo had little to fear from one or two wolves, they often watched in curiosity, thus allowing human hunters posing as wolves to get well within shooting range.

Indeed, I learned that the wolf and his virtues are still woven into the life and cultures of many contemporary native North American tribes. Among some Plains tribes, the Pawnee were known as the Wolf People. Those who are still familiar with Plains hand signs know that the sign for Pawnee is the same as the sign for wolf—the middle and index finger of the right hand upraised in a V-shape to the right of the head. Among my own people, one of the names for the Winter Moon (probably December) was also the Moon When Wolves Come Together, or *Mayaca Akimnaiciyapi Wi*. Knowing these kinds of cultural connections, I began to feel a kinship of spirit with the wolf and with the people of other tribes.

As a young man I learned the reason wolves and warriors no longer existed in my part of the world. The first peoples and the wolf had been driven to the brink of extinction by a newcomer to Turtle Island—the European.

Joseph Marshall III

The European labeled the first peoples Indians, and he carried with him an ancient, misbegotten hatred and fear of the wolf. He stepped onto our lands and brought with him the beginning of the end for both the first peoples and the wolf.

The European, it was easy to see, moved outside of the natural order of life, obviously having forgotten his origins. He was arrogant because of his ability to reason, seeing it as justification to be higher than other species. His approach to life in a world that was new only to him was to change it to suit his needs and limitations. Furthermore, he knew that the first peoples of Turtle Island were different from him, and he chose not to see beyond both real and imagined differences. Before long the European was driving wolves and Indians from their homes and killing them. In the 1600s in the New England area, bounties were offered and paid for both dead wolves and dead Indians.

The extent of the European's arrogance, his fear of the Indian, and his hatred of the wolf is evident in how swiftly he drove them away. In a little less than 370 years after he first stepped onto this continent, he had killed or driven off all of the wolves in the eastern half of what eventually became the United States of America. In an area containing 1.2 million square miles, there were nearly 77 million acres of land without a single wolf where previously there had been thousands upon thousands—perhaps hundreds of thousands.

By the same time, many Indian tribes in the East were extinct, mostly killed off by European diseases for which they had no natural immunities. Historians and ethnologists today are cautiously estimating that perhaps as many as ninety percent of the pre-European peoples of Turtle Island (North America) were wiped out by European diseases. While this kind of disease driven decimation of Indian populations was largely unintended, there seems to be no reliable documentation to suggest that Europeans substantially altered their patterns of contact with Indians to lessen the impact of diseases.

In the late 1800s, the wolf was slaughtered by the tens of thousands in the western mountain regions of the United States. By then many Indian tribes were already stagnating on reservations—areas of land that were (and are) a minute fraction of once vast territories. Shortly after the turn of the twentieth century, wolves were extremely rare below the forty-eighth parallel, after numbering an estimated two million in the 1600s; and the population of the first peoples was about two hundred thousand in comparison to the estimates of three to twenty million at the time of first European contact in the late 1400s.

The time span of this population decline may not seem noteworthy from the reference point of the average human lifespan or that of any other species. Four hundred years is a long time for any creature whose lifespan is less than one hundred years. But from the perspective of length of existence on Turtle Island, wolves have been here for two million years, and the first peoples for perhaps as long as sixty thousand. Furthermore, the starkly tragic realization should be that this population decline was a manifestation of unfettered enmity.

Commenting on European enmity toward the wolf, British writer Ewan Clarkson wrote in his 1975 book *Wolf Country* that "…no war waged by man against any species has been fought so long, or so mercilessly as his campaign against the wolf." Though that statement tragically has the ring of truth, I can only assume that Mr. Clarkson omitted—without intention—the first known human inhabitants of Turtle Island from inclusion in his definition of "species."

In the late 1800s, General Phillip Sheridan (in whose hands and heart rested the "Indian policy" of the United States and the futures of many Indian tribes) told a friendly Indian that "the only good Indians I ever saw were dead." That statement reflected a real attitude of the times, and it seems to be a latent sentiment that surfaces now and then. Though we Indians have been citizens of the United States since 1924, there are times we are still treated as a threat to non-Indian society. For example, the state of Wyoming is fighting a United States Supreme Court decision that awarded senior water rights to the Eastern Shoshoni and Northern Arapaho tribes within the exterior borders of their reservation. Likewise, many non-Indian Americans still cling to ancient myths from their European origins regarding the wolf as a beast of "waste and desolation," apparently to the extent of disregarding current law. A hunter who killed a wolf near Yellowstone National Park in 1992 was never prosecuted, although a federal law protects wolves as a threatened and/or endangered species with provisions for punishment of lawbreakers.

In a real sense, both the first peoples and the wolf are still endangered species. Our future is uncertain within the framework of American society.

On Behalf of the Wolf and the First Peoples

We are continually judged from the viewpoints of progress, technology, and vestiges of "manifest destiny" and are found wanting, or unwanted. Misinformation, misconception, arrogance, and just plain ignorance continue to be the factors at the core of such sentiment—all resulting in anti-Indian and anti–wolf attitudes reminiscent of nineteenth century beliefs. Such sentiments undoubtedly played a role in the refusal or unwillingness on the part of the states of Arizona, Maine, and New Mexico to allow Indians to vote. Arizona was forced by court decree to do so in 1948, while Maine dropped its ambiguous objections in 1954. In 1962 New Mexico had to be forced by the federal government to let Indians exercise their voting rights. In the mid-1960s, the state of South Dakota wanted to assume complete civil and criminal jurisdiction over Indian reservations, but a successful countercampaign by the United Sioux Tribes convinced voters to defeat the issue in a statewide referendum. If the referendum had passed, it would have effectively further eroded the sovereignty of eight Sioux tribes within the state.

Wolves are considered a direct threat to ranching, farming, and hunting lifestyles in the American West. Ranchers and farmers in Wyoming, Montana, and Idaho are opposed to wolves in Yellowstone National Park. At times I get the impression that they think that a pack of wolves will put them immediately out of business. It would be interesting and certainly illuminating to ascertain exactly how many farmers and ranchers have been forced out of business as a direct result of wolf

Joseph Marshall III

predation in areas of the United States and Canada where domestic livestock are in proximity to wolves.

Big game hunters and guides are mounting their own protest. They speak of the necessity of managing big game numbers and cry that wolves will kill too many elk and deer. The real concern, however, is that *wolf predation* might interfere with *human predation*. Thus, the hypocrisy in all of this is that hunters and guides decry the apparent "wantonness" and "pleasure" with which a wolf kills, while hiding their own lust for killing behind the arguments of the human hunter's sacred role in "game management."

Wolves apparently do have the ability to single-handedly drive ranchers, farmers, and big game guides out of business, and while denying the human hunter the pleasure of killing bighorn sheep, deer, moose, and elk, they can also take a bite out of the pocketbook of every unsuspecting ordinary citizen.

Indeed, much of the debate over wolves seems to focus on two basic issues: money and control. Consider the words of a seventy-six-year-old Montana rancher, commenting on the plan to reintroduce wolves to Yellowstone National Park (from a television documentary entitled *Return of the Wolves*): "Well, they spent a lot of money getting them controlled, I suppose fifty, seventy-five years [ago]…and nobody had no trouble until just recently, with these wolves. I can't see the reason for inviting them now. I can't see the advantage of it, really, myself."

Perhaps the fact that a certain amount of money was spent eradicating wolves from Yellowstone is reason enough for some not to reintroduce them, thereby obfuscating the possibility that eradicating them in the first place raises questions about man's ultimate arrogance regarding his place in the greater scheme of things. The expenditure of money should only be regarded for what it really is all too often: a quick, shallow, and convenient answer indicative of a philosophy bereft of insight, intellect, and morality. Further compounding this fact is that the rapid and magnanimous expenditure of money too often sanctifies the reason for it, no matter how ridiculous, self-serving political, ineffective, or brutal.

The concept of control is just as important as money and is of the "might makes right" school of thinking. Some examples of it are the "No Dogs or Indians Allowed" signs that were posted in many places of business throughout the central and northern Plains states in the 1930s, 1940s, and 1950s. I recall being with my parents and another Indian family at a Fourth of July fair and carnival in Martin, South Dakota, in the mid-1950s. After a parade, a voice over the loudspeaker reminded everyone that "no Indians were allowed on Main Street." As a young adult, I was reminded of that particular moment when I saw a cartoon depicting a white man in a cowboy hat commenting to an Indian, "I hear you Indians are trying to take over the reservation." For me, growing up on an Indian reservation meant having a substantial portion of my existence subject to non-Indian control, directly or indirectly. I was expected to speak English. I was expected to tacitly agree (or at least not disagree) when non-Indians ridiculed or condemned any aspect of my culture. Indian parents were expected to accept the fact

Joseph Marshall III

that non-Indian school boards, administrators, and teachers were indoctrinating Indian students with irrelevant curriculum, as well as displaying blatant insensitivity to the Indian culture which still existed; and then Indians were blamed for the high incidence of school dropouts. Control, then, meant having the power and ability to speak and act without sensitivity and with impunity. Recently, there have been positive and impactive changes, especially in the area of education for Indian students on Indian reservations. But those changes have come about largely because Indian parents and organizations initiated them after they had grown tired of being controlled.

A group that perceives itself to be better can exercise control over another group or groups considered to be lesser, often with the tacit approval of most segments of the controlling group. Sooner or later, the dynamic changes to protecting and perpetuating control, regardless of the issue or the cost. A case in point is Indian gambling.

Gambling appears to be an answer for the chronic lack of economic development on Indian reservations, not to mention an economic windfall for adjacent non-Indian communities. But states are scrambling to control Indian gambling, often citing as their rationale such things as morality or the fear of organized crime or wanting their fair slice of the pie. But the real reason for their scrambling is to maintain control of control, and Indians.

Indians, after all, were put on reservations to be controlled. Wolves were controlled through extirpation.

The first peoples of this continent and wolves have certainly faced the same difficulties. Our populations were decimated and our territories reduced drastically. And there are still difficulties for us to face. Mostly the whims of ignorance and arrogance. There is still racial prejudice against Indians and still an occasional cry to terminate reservations. The wolf is still the heavy in *Little Red Riding Hood,* in the animated children's movie *Beauty and the Beast,* in the feature film *White Fang,* and in the minds of misinformed people. All too consistently, somewhere into conversations about wolves and Indian creep the watchwords *control* and *in their places.* To some, we are acceptable only under certain conditions and circumstances. After all, the West was made safe for "civilization" because wolves were killed off and Indians were "conquered," not to mention that the land itself was "tamed." But the reality is that what does remain of the natural environment is not tame; and wolves and Indians are still here.

While the populations of the first peoples are mere fractions of what they once were, our societies are still basically intact. We are still here because we have persevered, enabled by our societal structures, values, and spirit. Ironically, those were the very things once considered antithesis to civilization—living with and within the parameters of nature instead of always contesting it, and knowing and understanding that every living organism contributes to the totality of life—these realities from the physical existence we all share may be the very things that save "civilization" from itself. And if not, then the hard lessons we have learned on the five

Joseph Marshall III

hundred-year road we have traveled certainly have earned us the right to say how it should not be done.

We—the wolf and the first peoples—have within us a key to the future of this country and, indeed, the world. A truth instilled by adversity. A truth both ancient and new.

Millenniums ago we both roamed freely. We did not destroy the land or contaminate the water or foul the air. Our populations did not exceed the physical world's ability to support us. We each had a place in the natural order, the Great Circle of Life, and we kept our places. Nor did we unduly or self-righteously interfere with any other species.

The new, more recent truth comes from having stood on the brink of extinction. It is simple and frightening. The actions, attitudes, and policies by which Indians and wolves are "controlled" are the same that are applied to the land, air, and water—actions, attitudes, and policies that have deep roots in arrogance, ignorance, and apathy when they should be based on truth, understanding, and compassion.

For the sake of the world, we pray that non-Indians and non-wolves will see these truths. And if these truths are seen and accepted, then we will all know that there is a natural order still, no matter how much we may have allowed technology and anthropocentrism to hide it from us.

We pray that all will learn that it ultimately does not matter whether we walk on four legs or two, fly, crawl, swim, or sink roots into the Earth—we are all the same, because we are given life, we live life, and then we die. As steadfastly as technology and human arrogance may try, that cycle will not be circumvented. The fact that we have split the atom or walked on the moon or generally dazzled ourselves with the apparent "miracles" of technology—such as test-tube babies, virtual reality, and cyberspace—has obscured a basic truth: unless and until we understand the simplest of realities, we should not think ourselves capable and responsible enough to understand the complex. And the simplest of realities is that no matter who or what we are or who and what we think we are, we all come from the Earth, and we will all return to the Earth. Realizing and accepting this one simple reality should help us begin to understand that technology can be a beneficial tool of intelligent compassion and not a pedestal from which to look down on everything and everyone else. No more than is being of a particular skin color, of a particular religious belief, of a particular social class, a particular gender, or a particular species.

We can take a lesson from the Dakota hunter and Woman Who Lived with the Wolves. We can share sustenance; we can go beyond individual physical and philosophical boundaries. We can learn that we can learn to coexist. We can learn that, in the long run, coexistence is preferable to dominance because dominance manifests itself through arrogance, anthropocentrism, racism, and just plain narrow-mindedness.

In the past, the wolf and the first peoples of Turtle Island lived and moved on the same earth. We coexisted. That did not necessarily mean that we were always pleased with one another. But it did mean that we always respected one another's right to be.

Joseph Marshall III

There are still moments when my spirit weeps for the wolves and the warriors who are gone. Fortunately, there are still wolves in the world, and in many like me flows the blood of ancient warriors. The blood of the first peoples. At this moment, the wolves have returned to Yellowstone National Park, to a place that once knew the voices and songs of their ancestors. They have returned because some two-leggeds have learned that there can be room for us all. On behalf of the wolf and the first peoples, I hope the lesson does not end in Yellowstone.

One night a few years ago the dream came again. Soon after, in the early summer of 1993, I drove during the dawn hours through the beautiful mountains in western Wyoming. I stopped my truck and walked to the edge of a bluff. In the cool, gray dawn, feeling particularly connected to everything around me, I lifted my face and sang the song of the wolf. A few heartbeats later, I thought I heard an answer from across the valley. Perhaps it was just the echo of hope.

Not All Indians Dance

Among non-Indians there continues to exist many misconceptions about Indians. Such misconceptions, I believe, are remnants of pre-twentieth-century European and Euro-American descriptions of and attitudes about Indians. Characterizations of Indians in seventeenth-, eighteenth-, and nineteenth-century non-Indian America were somewhat polarized. On the one hand Indians were considered the "children of nature," and on the other hand, they were seen as the "vilest miscreants of the savage race."

As "children of nature" ("noble redmen" was another popular epithet), we were accorded mystical and mysterious qualities because of our perceived or assumed abilities to "commune" with nature and to otherwise exist in an environment confusing and mysterious to Europeans. As "miscreants" and "savages," we were feared and detested; we "infested" the land along with bears and wolves in an environment feared and misunderstood by the newcomers.

Both descriptions stemmed from misinformation, ignorance, and myth—often given impetus by various writers of the day such as James Fenimore

Joseph Marshall III

Cooper and Francis Parkman. Parkman was especially fond of layers of desultory adjectives allegedly providing realistic images of Indian people and Indian life. But somewhere in between the polarized characterizations of Indians and Indian culture, steadfastly resisting the populist literary jibes of the Coopers and the Parkmans and their current versions, is the reality of what we were and are. This is a reality that non-Indians still have difficulty discovering and it is this difficulty, I believe, that prevents other Americans from perceiving us and interacting with as we are: human beings no better or worse than any other group of human beings.

All misguided and ill-founded opinions about Indians do us damage. However, the one that is often overlooked or even accepted because it seems to be less offensive—although ultimately, it is just as misleading and just as damaging—is the notion that Indians are or should be mystical and mysterious. When this assumption is connected to the notion that Indians are capable of "communing" with nature, sensible Indian approaches to relating to the natural environment are obscured. Although we did—and do—*commune* with nature, that communion is not based on mystical abilities but on our acceptance of the realities of the physical world; in short, we accepted the facts of what nature is and does. Our grasp of the fundamental realities of our environment—such as never setting up an encampment in a known and active floodplain—is obscured when anyone regards them as mystical or mysterious.

Several years ago, a friend who was an adopted child learned that his biological father was a Sioux

Indian. A subsequent search through records at several Sioux reservations in South Dakota eventually brought him to the Rosebud Sioux Reservation, and the knowledge that his father had been a Rosebud Sioux. My friend ended up working on the reservation. More importantly, though his biological father was dead, he found and established relationships with some of his blood relatives still living there.

As a result of his link with the reservation, my friend made a strong connection with part of his identity. His search for that identity and the resulting connection (or reconnection) was not a total surprise to him. "In a way," he told me, "my existence has been validated. And I'm not surprised at what I've learned about myself, because I've always loved nature."

I think, in part at least, my friend (not unlike many people these days) was a victim of an image of what an Indian should be. He was taught and therefore was loyal to the stereotype of the "noble red man" image. Being the kind of person he is, he wants to see the best in people, individually and collectively. Even before he learned of his own Indian identity, he questioned and resisted the image of the Indian as "savage" and readily embraced the more positive one.

I love my friend dearly. So although I sometimes wonder at his choice to leave the reservation, I do understand it. He had come to the Rosebud to learn something about himself and to make a connection. Having done those things, he came to a crossroads, and he chose to return to more familiar territory. Perhaps a small part of the reason was that the reality of being Indian on a reservation had finally changed the images

Joseph Marshall III

and stereotypes that had been unchallenged for so long in his mind. Yet something my friend said made me sad for him. I can still hear the disappointment in his voice and see a slight confusion in his eyes as he remarked, "I thought I would see an Indian behind every tree when I got here." Of course, he did not. I hope he understands that the failure of a stereotype to manifest itself does not diminish *his* "Indianness" or *his* identity. On the contrary, I think he is stronger because he has faced the reality of being Indian.

Three years ago I was interviewed on camera for a cable television program about the West. The segment was about the Oglala Lakota (Sioux) war leader Crazy Horse, one of the best-known Indian leaders to emerge from the turbulent years on the northern Plains in the latter half of the last century.

The segment producer had done his homework in preparation for the interview. His questions about Crazy Horse were appropriate, insightful, and calculated to elicit responses that would tell a cohesive, chronological story. At the conclusion of the interview, he asked if there was anything else I would like to add. My reply was, "Well, we could talk about how he [Crazy Horse] was a dead shot with a bow."

The young producer smiled politely and dismissed my comment with an offhanded remark, thereby ending the interview. He was more interested in the mystical aspects of Crazy Horse's life and times— the legend rather than the man. He could not be persuaded to talk about something so mundane as a Lakota warrior shooting a bow. But in refusing to do so, he totally disregarded a very human aspect of Crazy

Horse. There seem to be two approaches in all writings about Crazy Horse. One approach tends to establish and enhance the legend of Crazy Horse, and the other tends to diminish and distort his image and accomplishments. Neither approach is overly concerned that the legend was first a man a human being. However, if we want to know and understand Crazy Horse as a man, we must brush aside the veil of mystery and mysticism, because they stand between us and reality.

I wanted that young producer to know more about Crazy Horse. I wanted to describe the ordinary things that Crazy Horse did—things that helped define his identity and that are part of life for every Lakota man, woman, and child. I wanted to stress aspects of real life that contributed to his humanity—such as his grief over the death of his younger brother or his sense of guilt because a close friend and mentor was killed in battle before an intense disagreement between them had been reconciled. And nothing was more real or humanly mundane than Crazy Horse's lapse in judgment when he tried to steal another man's wife—a lapse in judgment that nearly cost him his life and did cost him a position of leadership.

If all of these events are not considered relevant to Crazy Horse's identity, then it is certainly because we are blinded by the *legend* of Crazy Horse. We see legends riding ahead of hundreds of warriors to lead an attack. We see legends riding up into the clouds on white horses. We see mysticism and mystery. But we miss seeing the man.

If we did see the man inside the legend, we would see that Crazy Horse was human enough to

Joseph Marshall III

weep at the deaths of a brother and a friend, human enough to allow his love and lust for a woman to destroy his judgment. We would see that the man inside the legend could shoot a bow with deadly accuracy, make a bow and arrows, tie his moccasin laces, pull his leggings on one leg at a time, feel the winter's cold, perhaps dread getting up in the morning, fall asleep on the back of a horse from bone-weary exhaustion, feel more than a little tinge of jealousy knowing that the woman he loved belonged to another man, or feel his stomach ball up in knots just before a battle.

All of this was what I wanted to tell the young producer about Crazy Horse. Sadly, the producer seemed to have been seduced by the legend and did not want to look behind what he perceived to be more appropriate and important—the aura of mysticism and mystery.

Two personal experiences may serve as examples of how Indians individually are sometimes stereotyped and thus abstracted. Four years ago, two friends and I drove several miles out from our homes in Casper, Wyoming, to take some pictures for an article I had written on primitive Lakota (Sioux) bows and arrows. After all the pictures were taken, I strung one of my bows, nocked an arrow, and shot it high into the air. After I returned from retrieving the arrow, one of my friends asked what I was doing. "Just shooting my bow," I told her. "Oh," she said, looking disappointed. "I thought you were doing something symbolic."

Another similar incident took place several years ago while I was still living on the Rosebud Sioux Indian Reservation. On this occasion, I went to watch the traditional dancing at the annual Rosebud Sioux Fair and Rodeo. I was attending the evening session, and as I walked to the bleachers under the arbor to find a good perch from which to watch the dancing, I found myself suddenly surrounded by a non-Indian family. They had a few questions.

Their questions were courteous and not unusual for people who were seeing Indians dancing up close and personal for the first time. I answered them the best I could and as courteously as they had been asked. It was my answer to their final question that provoked a most unusual reaction.

"When will *you* dance?" the man asked. "Oh, I don't dance," I replied. There was profound shock on five faces. Apparently, I had given the wrong answer.

"You don't dance?" the woman asked. It was more of a plea for me to change my answer.

"No," I said. "I don't dance."

"Do you sing?" asked one of the children.

"No," I replied again. "I don't sing."

"Why?" asked another of the children.

I shrugged. "Well," I said, "Not all Indians dance, and not all Indians sing."

They backed away from me and disappeared into the crowd, taking their shock and disappointment with them. Their reaction and the attitude that facilitated it is not unusual among non-Indians today.

For far too long, non-Indians (generally speaking) have approached us only so far. They will go to a powwow or buy a pair of moccasins or read a history book on Indian religion. They may tell themselves that they are "really getting into" Indian culture or history. In truth, they are more like the person who comes to a lake for a swim but only ends up walking around and around it, cautiously testing the water by sticking in a toe or a foot. In the end, the person does not swim because he is afraid that the water may be too cold or too deep.

Going to a powwow or buying a pair of moccasins brings you to the edge of the lake. Reading books about Indian history and religion is like sticking a toe or a foot into the water. If you do not go into the water, you'll never learn that there are living, breathing human beings beneath the feathers and inside the beaded buckskin dresses at the powwow—living, breathing human beings with a history and a variety of contemporary issues and concerns. Such as—

♦ One of the oldest man–made artifacts in North America is an approximately 27,000-year-old scraper found near Old Crow Flats in the Yukon Territory.

♦ The Oraibi Pueblo has been continuously inhabited for at least one thousand years, making it the oldest town in North America.

♦ In 1869, Ely Parker or Donehogawa, a Seneca, was the first Indian to be appointed United States Indian commissioner. Prior to that he was a brigadier general in the United States Army and was with General Grant at Appamatox when General Lee surrendered.

♦ The Iroquois Confederacy was a representative and deliberative body composed of six nations, within which women had a strong voice. Some scholars argue strongly that it was a direct influence on the shaping of the United States Constitution.

◆ Many current highways in the United States are ancient trails first used by Indians and, of course, later "blazed" by European and Euro-American explorers.

◆ All of the current surviving Indian nations in the United States are older than the United States.

◆ Charles Curtiss, vice-president under Herbert Hoover, was a Kaw Indian from Oklahoma. He was also the first Indian to serve in the United States Senate.

◆ The Bureau of Indian Affairs was established in 1824 within the Department of War.

◆ The Indian Health Service was established in 1955 and is now part of the Department of Health and Human Services.

◆ Indians were made citizens of the United States by an act of Congress in 1924.

◆ About eight thousand Indians, served in the United States armed forces in World War I, twenty-five thousand in World War II, twelve thousand in the Korean War, forty-five thousand in the Vietnam War, and one of the first American servicemen to die in Desert Storm was a Sioux Indian Marine from South Dakota.

◆ Eighteen United States Congressional Medals of Honor were awarded to soldiers of the United States Seventh and Ninth cavalries for their action at Wounded Knee in 1890.

Joseph Marshall III

◆ The Indian Reorganization Act of 1934 "gave"
Indian tribes the right to self-government.

◆ The concept of reservations for Indians
was born before the United States was born.

◆ There are 384 federal and 23 state reservations
in the United States.

◆ Virtually no reservation is a solid block
of Indian-owned or controlled land.
Most reservations have to contend with
substantial white land ownership within their
borders, which in turn is the basis for continuing
questions and problems regarding civil and
criminal jurisdiction.

◆ Twenty-six of the fifty state names are taken
from Indian names or words.
Including Texas and Indiana loosely
into that category raises the number
to twenty-eight.

◆ Thirty-one of the fifty states have at
least one Indian reservation, with California
having seventy-five. There are no
reservations in Oklahoma or Alaska.

◆ Two of the bigger issues facing
Indians today are gambling on reservations
and the location of nuclear waste
storage facilities on reservations.

◆ There are at least twenty-six Indian-founded
and controlled colleges on several reservations
across this country.

◆ At least twenty-seven non-Indian
institutions of higher learning offer
at least a major in Indian Studies.

◆ Sixty to seventy thousand Indian young people are now enrolled in college.

Of course, the list goes on and on, based on the interesting as well as tragic aspects of Indian history, rich and varied cultures and lifestyles, and the current issues and problems that face Indians day in and day out. Such information can be a source of insight and enlightenment into cultures that are old beyond remembering and peoples who have existed for millenniums.

Therefore, you can understand why it is so important for you to come into the water. If you don't, you may never see beyond the narrow viewpoint of the history books, which tend to ignore or slant Indian history. Then, the chances are that you will allow yourself to believe that we are more important as a part of the past—and keep us there in your mind—thereby denying and/or avoiding the fact that we are part of the present. If you don't come into the water, it will be easy and safe for you to lay that mantle of mystery and mysticism on us. Then you can always keep us at arm's length. You'll stick your toe in the water now and then, but you will never jump in. And in the end, we will all lose. Because we will never be anything more to you than objects of mystery and sources of "mysticism." You may well buy many pairs of Indian moccasins in your time, but you will never know how it feels to walk in them.

Shrugging off that mantle of mystery and mysticism is not an easy thing for us to do. Sometimes we are not allowed to do that, or even try. Like the tourist family that refused to believe that I do not dance, many non-Indians are loath to give up their myths when it comes to Indians. A further complication is that there is no single answer or solution. One size will not fit all. At the same time, we must not allow the complexity of the situation to obscure the fact that we are facing a basic human problem—a failure to communicate.

There is an anecdote that makes the rounds now and again that seems to aptly illustrate this dilemma.

A cowboy was looking to buy a horse and was told that a certain old Indian had several good horses for sale. The cowboy went to the Indian's place and was led into a corral full of horses. As he moved among the milling animals, he noticed one standing in a corner alone. It was a tall, good-looking, straight-legged sorrel. After sizing the sorrel up for several minutes, the cowboy announced that he wanted to buy him.

The old Indian protested. "He doesn't look so good," he advised.

The cowboy became impatient over such an obvious sales tactic. "You couldn't be more wrong, Chief," he said. "It is the best-looking one of the bunch."

The old Indian said once more, "He doesn't look so good."

The cowboy's insistence won out. He bought the sorrel, paid for him, saddled him, and rode away.

Just after sunset he returned to the Indian's corral, leading the sorrel. Horse and cowboy were limping. The man's clothes were torn, and he had an assortment of bumps and bruises. And he was angry.

"Chief!" the cowboy said. "This damn horse ran right off the edge of a cliff with me. Why didn't you tell me he was blind?"

The old Indian shook his head. "I did. I told you he doesn't look so good."

Communication is basically a two-way process. A failure to communicate is due to many reasons. Silence is the biggest factor. But, in my opinion, it is only slightly ahead of selective hearing.

Selective hearing is, obviously, hearing only what one wants to hear. We encounter that problem among some historians who are fearful of what they label "revisionist" history. They are fearful that revisionist historians are out to change history, but what they are really afraid of is that they (the old-line historians) may be forced to hear what they do not want to hear—both sides of the story or all of the facts.

For example, when the "Agreement" of 1875 is discussed, wherein Sioux (Lakota) leaders apparently yielded control of the Black Hills after the 1874 confirmation of the discovery of gold, it is referred to as a negotiated agreement. Historians fail to mention that the Sioux leaders were literally forced to agree due to the real threat of the immediate loss of annuities (food and supplies) and by immediate forced removal of the Sioux people to Indian territory in Oklahoma.

Sometimes historians simply fail to mention Indian involvement or contribution, such as the hundreds if not thousands of Indians who fought in the Civil War—on both sides.

The tourist family at the Rosebud Fair several years ago was not so much interested in whether or not I danced; rather, they were looking for an affirmation of a myth—that all Indians dance. They were not interacting with me as a person; they were trying to touch a myth. They did not want to hear that I do not put on feathers and dance; they did not want to face reality as it related to one Indian. It seemed to be easier for them to safely categorize all Indians. If they had allowed communication to occur on a person-to-person basis, they might have learned that there is more to being Indian than dancing.

I might have told them that, while I do not dance, I do speak my native (Lakota) language; in point of fact, it is my primary language. I might have told them that I make bows and arrows or that there are ancestral names like White Feather Tail, Uses Cane, Two Hawk, Good Voice Eagle, Blunt Arrow, Little Bird, Caught the Eagle, and even Morrison, Roubideaux, and McClean in my family tree. If communication had occurred, we would have met on common ground. I would have been able to shrug off the mantle of mystery and mysticism, and they would have been able to see past a myth. We would have met on the common ground of our humanity.

Personally, I do not enjoy being a myth. And I suspect that if Crazy Horse could speak to us now, he would implore us to remember him as a man and not as a legend. In other words, see me as I am. As a person, a human being. If you must judge me, judge me at that level. Do not judge me on the basis of an image or an idea that has long ago lost its connection to reality.

There is a general premise among many non-Indians that Indians are or should be mystical and mysterious. But that imposed aura of mysticism and mystery must be removed to find the real people, real values, real traditions, real history. Indians are sometimes mundane and sometimes ordinary, sometimes fascinating, but always very human and very real. Given a choice, I'd much rather be mundane and ordinary than a vile miscreant.

Finally, although it is frequently non-Indians who stereotype Indians as mystical or mysterious, we must all understand that debunking such stereotypes is a two-fold task. If we Indians do our part, we will teach our fellow Americans that there is not an Indian behind every tree, or that everything we do is not symbolic, and that not all Indians dance. All of which is as it should be and probably always was. And by the way, did I mention that about 145 Indian languages are still spoken in the United States?

Joseph Marshall III

If Only the Hunter Were Equal to the Prey

I am a hunter, an archer, and a Native American. There was a time on Turtle Island (North America) when one of those labels automatically included the other two. Now one must be careful about admitting to being any of the three. Furthermore, one can now be any of the three without a clue as to what the other two are about. To further complicate the situation, people are sometimes confused when I mention that I am a bow hunter. The revelation sometimes needs to be followed with the explanation that I do not hunt bows, I hunt with a bow. As a matter of fact, primitive bows have been part of my life since early boyhood. Therefore, while as a Native American I am part of an ethnic and numerical minority, I am more so as a primitive bow hunter and bowyer.

The (at least) 10 million archers in the United States today far outnumber the 2 million Native Americans counted in the 1990 Census. It is difficult to estimate how many Native Americans today are involved in any form of archery. Not very many, I suspect. And it is a safe bet that even fewer have any historic and cultural knowledge of archery specific to their particular tribes. Fewer still are Native Americans who have the knowledge and skill to actually handcraft bows and arrows. Those I personally know who fit in the last category, I can count on less than the fingers of one hand. One assumes and hopes that there are more than that somewhere.

I suppose that, considering the number and kinds of issues facing Native Americans today, agonizing over the lack of traditional, primitive Native American archers, bowyers, and arrowsmiths is not a high priority to most of us. Primitive Native American archery is now thought of as outdated, outmoded, archaic, and unnecessary. Its loss is apparently not as drastic as the loss of a language. And considering all that we have lost—several hundred entire tribes, several hundred languages, over 2 billion acres of land, burial grounds, cultural artifacts, sovereignty, and so on—bows and arrows and primitive archers do appear to be a minor loss. But the loss of (or the change in) one part of a culture is rarely minor, because it almost always has larger ramifications. In this case, in addition to losing the knowledge of bows and arrows and how to make and use them, we have also lost the primitive hunter and his knowledge and definition of hunting. Gone is his comprehensive awareness of the life and death interrelationships of the natural environment. The awareness that a tree must die so that it can be crafted into a bow, so that as a bow it can be used to take the life of a deer, and that the deer dies so that the hunter and his family might eat and live. Gone is the sense of physical and spiritual connection to that cycle, which was the basis for a profound respect for the totality of life.

The activity called "hunting" today is referred to as a "sport." Today's "sport of hunting" is also a multimillion dollar industry. Today's archer uses a bow made of cables, pulleys, and space-age materials to launch arrows that are hollow aluminum, graphite, or fiberglass tubes. All of that only remotely resembles my definition of hunting and my knowledge of bows and arrows.

I do understand that things change. Institutions, traditions, customs, philosophies, languages, and so on, do evolve. There are not many things within the parameters and totality of our global existence that do not change or evolve. Even a river changes its course; and a mountain cannot remain unaffected by the change of seasons, freezing cold, merciless heat, and the inexorable passage of time. Change is undeniably a part of our existence. However, that should not mean that everything must change or that change is justified for the sake of change. Furthermore, we overlook or forget the inherent danger in change: it may not always bring about improvement.

Technology is change, technology brings change, and technology is seductive. More to the point, the rapidity of modern technological advances is seductive. If we accept every change, each "improvement," it is not long before we have completely forgotten the origins of an idea, a practice, or the original forms of a tool, utensil, or weapon. To forget or to have never been aware of origins deprives us of important aspects of ourselves, how we existed and functioned, and how we felt about the world around us.

Joseph Marshall III

A microcosm of that depravation happens when a typical modern archer acquires a bow. The first connection most modern archers have with the bow they shoot is when they purchase it. Their only investment is money, and many have no idea how the bow was made or what materials went into its construction. On the other hand, a primitive bowyer invests much more than money into a bow that he or she makes by hand. It begins with the kind of wood he or she chooses to use—to finding it, harvesting it, seasoning it, and finally seeing and feeling it take shape because of his or her knowledge and crafting skills. The process puts the bowyer in touch not only with the origin of one particular bow but of bows in general; and it can be the foundation for a genuine appreciation of what bows are all about. Modern archery only superficially resembles its origins, and some modern archers have been seduced into forgetting that bows can be made of wood and were, in fact, originally only of wood.

Technology is constantly changing the face of modern archery—so much so that "modern" archery of the 1940s appears primitive in comparison to today. Its attendant hype saturates the marketplace with images, uses, ingeniousness, and indispensibility of each new device designed to make us better archers—until the next innovation comes along in a few weeks or a few months and renders its predecessor obsolete.

Modern archery has effectively convinced its proponents and practitioners that without its vast and imposing array of gadgetry—pin sights, release aids, range finders, hydraulic bow stabilizers, and so forth—

one cannot be a good archer. In fact, gadgets seem to be the prerequisite for modern-day archery rather than a steady hand and a good eye. Gadgetry has also imbued its disciples with a sense of superiority, causing them to cast a condescending eye toward primitive and traditional archers. That is a less obvious but no less impactive change. Part of the reason that gadgets have found such a niche in modern archery is because they already have a niche in modern society in general—such as radar detectors (a.k.a. "fuzzbusters"), garage door openers, TV and VCR remote controls, cellular telephones, and cordless razors, to list but a very few. And in the same way that an archer who shoots a compound bow often casts a jaundiced eye toward a fellow archer who shoots a longbow, those who have gadgets sometimes regard those without as less fortunate or "not with the program."

During a recent search and buy foray into a department store, "I observed a father telling his young son that he did not have a VCR as a child. The boy was astonished and looked at his father with a mixture of disbelief and pity. "Wow, Dad! What did you do?" he asked.

If modern archers and bow hunters can generally disdain primitive or traditional archers, it is an easy step to look with even more scorn at game animals. Bow hunting—and hunting in general—then takes on a different meaning because the attitude guiding the hunter has changed. If he has not imprinted or imbued himself into the crafting of the weapon with which he pursues the animal, his perception of his link to that animal is limited only to one who can kill and one who

Joseph Marshall III

48

can be killed. Attitude is one facilitator of change. And it also is affected by change. Sometimes, it is a victim of change when the result is more harmful (negative) than remedial (positive). The glut of technology in archery today has victimized it and affected the attitudes of modern archers toward hunting. If hunting becomes a victim, then so does man himself. Hunting has long been a part of man's nature as a predator. However, no other predator has redefined hunting—only man. He has redefined hunting because of the effect of technology on his attitude toward it. In fact, like modern archery, modern hunting bears little resemblance to its origins. And unavoidably caught up in the wake of this change is man's attitude toward his fellow species on this planet.

It can probably be argued that, in the broadest definition, technology includes the primitive tools and weapons with which early man worked and hunted. Therefore, attitudes were affected when stone projectile points replaced sharpened sticks, when the atlatl replaced the spear, or when the bow replaced the atlatl. However, those changes occurred over thousands of years and not every few years or even months; and each new and improved weapon (or tool) was still individually handcrafted and not mass-produced. There was still a personal connection to each weapon, not only due to the meticulous handcrafting process but also because of the specific knowledge of the natural materials used to make it. Such knowledge and such investment of time and skill did not set the craftsperson, as hunter, apart or above the hunting process. It continually reaffirmed his role in and connection to the cycle of life and death. Weapons may have improved, but attitudes about hunting remained fundamentally unchanged.

In order to understand how hunting has changed, we need to have a basic grasp of what it was. We need to understand how tribal societies defined and used the activity of hunting. Since I have some insight into the primitive, nomadic hunting cultures of the Plains of Turtle Island, we shall examine that perspective.

To Live by Hunting

Hunting ceased to be a way of life for the Plains tribes once reservations were established. But millenniums and generations prior to reservations, hunting was a way of life. Crazy Horse, the Oglala Lakota (Sioux) leader, aptly described the cultural significance of hunting when he said, " you tell us to work for a living, but the Great Spirit did not make [create] us to work, but to live by hunting."

Hunting was part of survival. It was making a living. Its significance and necessity dictated the structure of tribal societies on the Great Plains. Obviously, someone had to hunt, and though both males and females knew how to hunt, the societal role of *hunter* was relegated predominantly to males. In fact, it was one of the two primary roles and responsibilities preordained for males. The other being *warrior.* The two roles were so integrated that a man could not be one without the other. In fact, it would be more appropriate to describe the basic role of the male in many Plains tribes as that of *hunter/warrior.* Let us examine the hunter half of the dual role of hunter/warrior and his contribution to the survival of family, community, and nation.

The ancient hunter of the Plains was a naturalist, a craftsman, an expert marksman, and a philosopher.

The Hunter as a Naturalist

As naturalist, the Plains hunter learned as much as possible about animals and the land, both generally and specifically. For example, he would acquire a basic awareness of the habits and habitats of a given species, such as deer. The hunter would know that deer are nocturnal feeders, have a tendency to bed down and remain in one area during daylight hours, and possess immeasurably keen senses of hearing and smell. He would also know that buck (male) deer are sometimes less cautious during the rut (breeding time).

Specific knowledge would narrow to a particular group or herd of deer. The hunter would know their favorite range, down to exact boundaries and landmarks. Long and patient observation would teach him how the herd tended to move about within that range, where and when they usually went for water, where they bedded down in the daylight hours, and even the individual propensities of individual members of the herd.

The hunter combined his knowledge of the deer with what he knew about the land. He knew where he could do a stalk (sneak up to within bow range) and where it was better to set up an ambush (hide and wait for deer to pass within bow range). He knew from which direction it was best to enter a draw or a canyon when the wind was blowing. From one year to the next, he knew where the best forage and shelter would be for the deer according to each season.

All of his general and specific knowledge increased his chances of bringing down a deer. It did not guarantee a kill, but without it, there was no chance at all.

Of course, knowledge and information about game were not limited to only deer. It included everything from cottontails to bison. Furthermore, hunting was certainly not a seasonal activity because it was necessary to continuously provide a family with the basic requirements of food, shelter, and clothing.

The average family could consume anywhere from a few hundred pounds to a few thousand pounds of meat each year. They would require forty to sixty deer and elk hides a year for clothing as well as personal and household items. Understandably, the hunter needed far more then good luck to provide for his family.

The hunter's awareness and knowledge relative to game animals and the land were the keys to his success. That critical knowledge was given to him by the previous generation of hunters in his family and community, and it was supplemented and enhanced by his own experiences. He, in turn, passed it on to the next generation. Furthermore, the hunter's intimate knowledge of the animals he pursued was the basis for sincere respect for their ability to fit into and survive in the total environment. In some cases, he even adopted

Joseph Marshall III

a certain animal habit or characteristic he found to be helpful in his own existence and survival—such as the ability of some birds to lure a predator from their nests or their young by feigning injury, or a young deer's ability to hide in plain sight by remaining absolutely motionless.

The Hunter as a Craftsman

Knowledge of game was critical for the procurement of basic necessities supplied by small and large game animals. Equally as critical were the devices with which the hunter trapped or killed the game.

The tools of the hunter's trade were traps, snares, and weapons. There were several types of these, all ingeniously constructed and employed.

Traps and snares ranged from something as simple as a slip knot attached to a spring device (such as a bent sapling), a balanced log or rock ready to fall when the supporting, balanced trigger stick was touched, or a concealed pit. Not only was it necessary for the hunter to know how and where to set snares or traps, he also had to know how to manufacture them by hand, sometimes without the benefit of tools.

The size of the prey, the terrain of its habitat, and the resources (raw materials) available were all factors that determined the kind of trap or snare that should be used. A good hunter did not usually carry traps or snares with him or even materials for their construction, except perhaps cordage. Instead, he relied on whatever material was at hand to construct the trap or snare on site. And concealed pits were used time and again, sometimes from one generation of hunters to the next.

Any device not a trap or a snare was a weapon. Hunting weapons included a curved hardwood throwing stick (often called a rabbitstick), a sling, a lance, and a bow and arrows. (Since I am limiting this discussion to the tribal cultures of the Plains immediately prior to the coming of the European, I have not listed the spear throwers, also called an atlatl. That device was, of course, used widely throughout Turtle Island before the development of the bow.) Variations of each of these weapons existed from tribe to tribe. In addition, some tribes adapted the lance and the arrow for spearing fish.

The manufacture, preparation, and use of traps and snares was done with great care. However, the manufacture of the weapons of hunting was done with greater care and precision.

Every hunter had a basic knowledge of the materials as well as the basic skills to produce all of his own weapons. In other words, he knew how to locate, harvest, and prepare raw materials for manufacture. Then using his crafting skills, he transformed the raw materials into durable and effective weapons. Some of those crafting skills were making rawhide; separating sinew into thread; making cordage from sinew and fibrous plant materials; making bowstrings from sinew and rawhide; carving, shaving, whittling, and bending wood; splitting feathers for fletching; flaking blanks from flint, chert, or obsidian in order to knap arrow or lance points; making glue; and wrapping on stone points and fletching with sinew.

Joseph Marshall III

54

Such specific knowledge of natural materials and the precise skills developed over many years by the hunter as a craftsman were the basis for a spiritual connection to his environment. As one who handcrafts primitive weapons, I can attest that it is nearly impossible to hold in one's hand something that once was alive and not feel a kinship to it. An awareness of that kinship certainly motivates one to make the best arrow or bow or knife that one's skills can produce.

Some weapons were not difficult or complicated to make, such as a rabbitstick or a sling. Lances were also relatively simple. The most difficult weapons to make and use were bows and arrows. (For a specific discussion on crafting bows and arrows see the essay, "On Making a Bow.")

The Hunter as a Marksman

Even the strongest, most beautifully made weapon was no guarantee of success for the hunter. Just as basic knowledge and skill were necessary to make weapons, so too was a basic level of skill necessary to use them effectively. The only way for the hunter to develop that skill was to practice constantly with every weapon in his arsenal. That process began when he was still a child and continued throughout his life.

The level of marksmanship a hunter attained corresponded to the amount of time he devoted to practice. The more practice, the higher the skill. The higher the skill, the deadlier the weapon. It was said that some hunters could consistently hit a cottontail rabbit at twenty paces with a rabbitstick or a sling and at twice that distance with a bow and arrow. In fact, there was a saying among the Lakota that aptly describes this aspect of the hunter: "A man will be as good as he will be with a bow only when he dies."

Among many Plains tribes the development of the young males into proficient hunters as well as formidable warriors was accomplished primarily through the one-on-one mentor system. That is, each boy had one mentor and teacher at a time, though he had several different ones over the course of his life. One of the best ways to motivate and teach a young person was by example. Insofar as weapons proficiency, especially marksmanship, was concerned, the budding hunter was consistently given a higher level to strive toward. No matter how skilled he became with a bow, for example, his mentor and teacher was always better. That superior skill of the teacher was always the next level to be achieved. Marksmanship was that important. Without it the hunter could not provide for his family. It was said that the family of a poor hunter was thin and poorly dressed because he could not hit what he aimed for. On the other hand, the family of a good hunter was well fed and well clothed because he could.

The Hunter as a Philosopher

The mature hunter knew his limitations and strengths as a human being. He was aware of the place he had relative to other forms of life. He was not the strongest or the swiftest or the weakest. He did not have the eyesight of the eagle, the speed of the antelope, the brute strength of the bear, or the endurance of the wolf. Indeed, every animal he hunted had at least one ability that could be used to outwit and elude him. Yet he did not consider himself as inferior because he knew that his special ability to reason was his equalizer—his speed, his strength, his special defense. At the same time, he also understood that this ability did not make him superior to other species because without it he certainly would be inferior.

When the hunter took to the forest or the plain with a weapon in his hands in pursuit of a deer or a buffalo, he under- stood that he was doing so in pursuit of life, so that he and his family might eat and live. He knew that others hunted as well, such as the eagle, the wolf, the mountain lion, the coyote, and the fox. And though some others were not hunters in the same sense, such as the buffalo or elk, their survival, their pursuit of life, meant the death of living things—grasses, shrubs, and small trees. Therefore, the human hunter did not think of his pursuit of life as more important relative to all other forms of pursuit happening around him. His was but one of many. Nor did he think that his pursuit, his hunt, was a way to demonstrate prowess or skill. Although those attributes were necessary for him to be a successful hunter and provider, he did not kill simply to prove he was good at it.

The hunter also understood that all life was sacred. Because everything had a place and a purpose, it was, therefore, worthy of acknowledgment and respect. The mature hunter did not chortle in victory whenever he brought down his prey, whether it was a rabbit or a buffalo. Because everything lived for a particular purpose, he knew that taking that life must also serve a purpose—not because he, as a man, had any priority to take life, but because he understood that he could be taken and used as well. Many hunters would leave an offering—tobacco ties, a bundle of sage, pieces of their own flesh—as atonement for the life they had taken. Sacred life, sacred meat.

The hunter once hunted to provide for the survival of his family. He hunted to provide food, shelter, and clothing, and every part of each animal he killed was put to use. He killed because he was a provider, not because he was a killer.

Today, we have "hunting seasons." We "manage" our game herds, not so much for the welfare of the game, but so we can have enough to shoot the next "hunting season." Hunting has become a ritual of machismo and braggadocio. It is symbolized by expensive weaponry mass-produced by others, mounted trophies, flourescent orange, and empty beer cans left on remote mountain trails. In short, we have redefined hunting. Most of us today cannot name the parts of any weapon, much less make our own.

We practice shooting for a few days before we take to the wilderness, paying a guide to put us within range of an animal we think of mainly as a target. We kill because we can, not because it is necessary for the survival of our families. We do not feel or demonstrate respect for any animal we kill, except for the size of its antlers, or the condition of its hide, or the number of points it scores so that it can be listed in the record book. We feel no reverence for its life or that it was a part of all life. To some, it really had no purpose until it was killed with a brand-name gun shooting the hottest bullet on the market and then was mounted and given glass eyes and hung on a wall as a testament to a five hundred-yard shot. There is no more sacred meat.

I know that many who do what is called hunting today try to do it ethically. Even so, many of them have no concept of or connection to what hunting once was. I think that every hunter, whether he or she hunts with a bow or gun, should experience at least one hunt with the most primitive form of his or her weapon.

Modern bow hunters should put aside their compounds and pursue game with a longbow, a recurve, or—better yet—a handcrafted Indian flatbow, along with wood arrows, of course. Gun hunters should take to the field with a black powder, single-shot muzzleloader. Perhaps in this way the modern "hunters" will shed their sense of arrogance and superiority. Perhaps they may learn that there is more to "hunting" than putting the crosshairs of a ten-power scope on a deer or elk at three hundred yards. That it is possible that real hunting requires much more than expensive weapons and gadgetry. In fact, they may learn that it requires none of those things.

Real hunting requires that the hunter be equal to the prey. To put it another way, the hunter must be worthy of his prey. But our technology-induced and -enhanced arrogance has destroyed that basic truth. The state-of-the-art spotting scope and the high-caliber rifles many of us carry into the woods certainly do set us apart from the deer and the elk. Sadly, too many of us think they set us above. We think we have a right to kill animals because we can—because killing is made easier and easier with technology. Technology and arrogance have destroyed the atavistic connections to hunting and turned us into killers.

Five years ago I went bow hunting for antelope south of Casper, Wyoming, in an area called Shirley Basin. I have two distinct memories of that hunt. First, there were several groups of gun hunters in the area. One out-of-state group was being driven around in a four-wheel-drive vehicle. As soon as a herd of antelope was spotted, the vehicle stopped and disgorged its cargo. The hunters began firing away at the antelope some three hundred yards from them. I heard about a dozen shots and saw two does go down. My second memory is of a lone doe.

She came down off a hill and was passing in front of my hiding place at no more than fifteen yards. I realized it would be an an easy shot. I pulled up my bow. But when she came even with me, she stopped and looked directly at me. I could see, mostly in her soft brown eyes, that she was an old doe—an old lady.

I spoke to her. "Grandmother," I said. "You have lived a long time. I will not be the one to end your life. Go and hide from the others." She turned and walked down into a narrow gully, and I never saw her again.

I have thought of that moment and that old doe many times since that day three years ago. It would have been easy to kill her, but I did not. Two people ridiculed me for it when I told them. But her flesh and her death were not necessary for the survival of my family. And though I was, for that day, a good enough hunter to

Joseph Marshall III

have positioned myself for a kill, I chose not to be a killer. And, for a brief moment, I lifted myself to her level. I was equal to my prey.

Hunters of the past were not superheroes. They did not possess a magical insight into their environment. They were not "children of nature." Instead, they were observers of nature and participants in its cycles. They participated in life on a philosophically equal footing with everything around them. They understood that their responsibility to clothe and feed their families did not preclude respect for those whose flesh provided those necessities. There was a very real respect for the sanctity of every life, be it a salmon, a deer, a sage hen, a seal, a rabbit, or an elk. Indeed, as my grandfather said in voicing an ancient philosophy: "The hunter lives for the hunt, but not for the kill."

My grandfather's words still ring true for me. I have hunted with both bow and gun, many more times with the bow. Those times when I did actually bring down what I was hunting are memories colored with regret. A visit to those memories is always accompanied by a request for forgiveness. And sometimes I think that such and such a hunt would have been perfect had it not been for the kill.

People who hunt these days have little awareness of traditional archers, bowyers, arrowsmiths, and Native Americans. But those of us who are any one or more of these represent a connection to origins. Origins that have been obscured by an illusion of superiority created by technology. Origins that we should never forget, because they can still teach us that being equal to our prey is an honor, not an insult. The spotting scope that helps us to find that deer or elk, the scope on the rifle that helps us to aim from longer and longer distances, and the high-powered rifle with an effective killing range measured in hundreds of yards are all tools that exponentially increase our chances to kill game. While they do enable us to be better "hunters" in terms of game harvest, they do not make us superior beings. If you think you are a superior being, then go after that same deer and elk *without* those aids.

The same premise can be applied to the archer who takes to the field or the woods with a compound laden with all of the up-to-the-minute accessories and gadgets. While hunting with a compound may or may not make hunting easier than hunting with a recurve, longbow, or a primitive bow, the array of gadgetry is like a magic wand seems to sprinkle its users with a noticeable dose of arrogance. Arrogance is the foundation for a sense of superiority, which often seduces one into thinking that what one is at the moment is better than anything that has been previously. Technologically speaking, perhaps, but certainly not attitudinally or philosophically. In order for anyone to have a comprehensive awareness of where and what and who one is at the moment, there must be an awareness of how it all began—an awareness of origins. To put it another way, one's perception of the moment and one's vision into the future are enhanced by how far one is willing to look into the past.

Primitive and traditional archers, bowyers, arrowsmiths, and Native Americans are rare these days. So are real hunters. But one does not have to be any of the above to have an awareness of origins. You can be a nonhunter or you can be a hunter with or a bow and outfit yourself with the latest array of gadgets and still have a profound respect for the environment within which you hunt and for the animals you pursue.

Unless conditions on this continent change drastically and very suddenly, hunting will still be seasonal for most of us, and it will still be regarded as a sport. Those who hunt will still take to the fields and forests with their choice of weapons and, perhaps, an undefinable feeling or urge that drives them to do so. Many of us will never completely understand that urge, that feeling that seems to come from deep within our beings. But some of us know that it exists in us because we are part of all life and not apart from it. It comes from the predatory instinct that flows in the blood of the raptors and predators of the world. An instinct that drives us to the chase. An instinct that makes us hunters.

In the beginning, since we did not have the slashing talons of the hawk, the fangs of the wolf, the claws of the mountain lion, we sharpened wooden spears, then knapped and attached stone points, then propelled shafts with the atlatl, then made bows, and then guns. Somewhere in the process, as our weapons became more complicated and more effective, we began to feel superior. We allowed our technology to give us an illusion of superiority. An illusion that obscured our origins. An illusion that changed us from hunters into arrogant killers.

The next time you take to the fields or the forests and that undefinable urge drives you to the chase, remember that it is this feeling that connects you to origins older than memory. Do not let that weapon in your hands, however simple or complex, however modern or ancient, break your connection to those origins. If you do not, then and only then can you truly call yourself a hunter. Only then can you be equal to your prey.

Joseph Marshall III

An Indian Viewpoint of History

The title of this discussion is not meant to imply that all Indians share the same viewpoint about history. As a group we have many divergent and, sometimes, diametrically opposed viewpoints about the same issues. However, the majority of us who have an interest in history in general or are concerned with our own specific tribal histories seem to share an opinion: that there is an Indian side to the history of this continent and that its total human history is not always told fairly or completely. Thus, the title.

My first vivid lesson about history came from my maternal grandfather. My mother had acquiesced to her parents raising her firstborn (which was not unusual among Indian families) and thus added a dimension to my world I might not otherwise have known. Childhood with my grandparents was a romp through the hills, river valleys, and prairies near our home just south of the Little White River in the northern part of (what was still then) the Rosebud Sioux Indian Reservation. It was also a formative journey through family and tribal stories, their sense of

Lakota culture and identity, and their perception and interpretation of what the Lakota world once was.

It is difficult to say which world and time was the most enjoyable, but it is not difficult to admit that both shaped who and what I am now. I learned from both grandparents that the present is given form and substance by the past, but it was my grandfather who revealed a basic truth about human history.

My grandfather would take me on walks. Sometimes we probed the draws leading down to the river. Sometimes we wandered (seemingly) aimlessly over the open, grass-covered prairie. Other times we followed the meandering river. He would point out soapweed, blue and gray sage, a meadowlark's nest, a matted circle of grass where a deer had spent the day, a spider's web in the forks of a dead plum shrub, an eddy near a slight bend in the river where the bullhead fishing would be good, the wary stare of a coyote from just beyond the crest of a hill, or how the wind could coax every blade of grass in a meadow to bend and sway in unison.

Every walk, every outing, was an adventure and an opportunity to learn, whether it was something about where the biggest buffaloberries grew or where the government used to pasture the beef-issue cattle with their U.S. brands. Thus I was able to see the land not only for what it was and what it offered, but also for what had happened on it with regard to the Lakota and the whites.

One day as we came back up from the river, he paused and told me to look at the trail we had walked. He did this several times until we gained the top of the hill. "Remember this trail," he said, "and all the trails you have walked, because someday I will send you back on your own. If you do not remember, you will lose your way."

Since then I have learned that there are many trails left on the land. Some are physical scars, and others are spiritual imprints. I have also learned that the land itself means different things to different people.

I do not know if my grandfather knew he was teaching me about history at that particular moment in the summer of my sixth year. I certainly did not know it then, but when I retraced the trails of my childhood memories, I found the lesson and the truth that was there. If I had not gone back the way I had come, I would not have learned a basic truth about history. If I had not remembered the trail, I would, in a sense, be lost today.

History is a trail that was walked by our ancestors. For us to know it and them, we must retrace it, look at it honestly and perceive it realistically, and then tell it factually. History is meaningful and multidimensional with this process. Without it, history is merely a story and sometimes an uninteresting one at that.

One of the most persistent historical anecdotes that I recall during elementary school was the one about George Washington and the cherry tree. It was, to be sure, a lesson about the character and integrity of someone popularly thought of as the "father" of this country. (In a nonhistorical context it could be a solid lesson about honesty if the story were factual.) But did a young George Washington really

Joseph Marshall III

chop down a cherry tree and then later freely admit his transgression? If not, why was the incident presented as fact?

Similarly, Daniel Boone is credited with "blazing" trails. It is a fact that he (and several others) in 1775 were hired to "open" a route from the Shenandoah Valley through the Cumberland Gap to the Ohio Valley. It is probably also a fact that the route laid out by Boone, called the Wilderness Road, was before then never used by whites. Boone, therefore, did "blaze" a trail new to whites. But given that the territory along and through which he laid out the Wilderness Road had been occupied and/or certainly known to the pre-European, indigenous inhabitants, Daniel Boone was not the first human to have "blazed" a trail in that area. However, even when white historians did not outright say so, they certainly implied that Daniel Boone laid out a trail where no human had ever walked before. This mind-set points to at least two European viewpoints of that time: Indians were not regarded as human, and Indians were not entitled to or did not have a history.

Being Lakota I was, as a young person, naturally and primarily interested in the history of my particular people. My grandparents and others of their generation were the original source of information and insight into Lakota history, culture, tradition, values, and language. From that foundation it was an easy step to learn about the Cheyenne, Crow, Arikara, Omaha, Blackfeet, Arapaho, Shoshoni, Hidatsa, Kiowa, Pawnee, Mandan, and several other tribes.

My grandparents and those of their generation with whom I came in contact did not all have the same specific historic information, though they did basically agree regarding tradition, values, and customs. However, as a group or a community, they possessed composite, anecdotal information, some of which could definitely be labeled empirical, since a few of the older ones had actually been present at events such as the Battle of the Greasy Grass (Little Bighorn) River or participated in the Ghost Dances. All of these older ones were certainly of the first generation to live on reservations and see their children born on the reservation. Most, on the other hand, were those very children. Each and every one, of both generations, was a repository of information. From that part of my childhood I remember many memorable moments and many stories, but I have two regrets: that it was over too soon and that I did not pay closer attention.

Some of the stories that I heard as a child were about something now known as the *Oregon Trail* but called the *Holy Road* by the storytellers. It was not until high school history that I was to understand that the Oregon Trail and the Holy Road were the same, both physically and as an occurrence.

Learning about the Oregon Trail was, for me, similar in many ways to learning about Daniel Boone or George Washington and the cherry tree. Learning about it was necessary, I was told, because it was essential to know *our* history. But I, as a Lakota, was not included in the collective *our* when the story of the Oregon Trail was unfolded before me. It was a totally one-sided story of white people, and for a time it cast a shadow of doubt on what I had learned about the Holy Road—until I realized that I was looking at two sides of the same story.

Joseph Marshall III

70

White American historians tout the Oregon Trail phenomenon as the greatest human migration in North America. It lasted about twenty years from the early 1840s to the early 1860s. Characterized as a necessary aspect of a growing nation, ordained by divine providence, and heroic, it certainly did occur. That is the one inescapable fact—along with all of its consequences—that thousands of people and many, many nations *other than white Americans* still live with today.

The trail itself was really a wide corridor along which the white emigrants traveled, originating primarily at Independence, Missouri. Other starting points were Saint Joseph, Missouri, and Council Bluffs, Iowa. The route moved in a generally northwesterly direction through northeast Kansas, from southeast to northwest Nebraska, a meandering course through southern Wyoming, southern Idaho, and on into northern Oregon, terminating at Oregon City in extreme northwest Oregon. In all it was roughly 2,100 miles long, although those who took the Applegate Cutoff Trail from southern Idaho down into northern Nevada, through extreme northern California, and then up through western Oregon to Oregon City might have traveled a bit further. For a period of twenty years white emigrants moved along this corridor mostly with ox- and horse-drawn wagons. Some pulled or pushed handcarts, and others simply carried their belongings.

Most of the teachers in whose classrooms I learned about the Oregon Trail extolled the white "pioneers" who "followed their dreams" and "built a nation." They talked about the courage, strength, sense of purpose, and ingenuity with which those emigrants overcame the "insurmountable" hardships of extreme weather conditions, sickness, famine, the raw and "untamed" land, and Indians.

The white American version of the Oregon Trail represented Indians as anything but flesh and blood people. We were listed with all of the other challenges and obstacles that had to be overcome by white fortitude and ingenuity. If the land could be tamed, the rivers crossed, hardships endured, and obstacles overcome, then the Indians could be "conquered." Or generally faced and confronted by intrepid white pioneers and bested by superior physical and mental ability, and better weaponry. There were many moments during which, as I sat outnumbered by mostly white classmates, I felt very lonely.

Loneliness, however, is not the only consequence of a one-sided history. For Indians who are forced to accept only the white version of a story, there is the constant danger of doubt about one's identity, both individually and collectively. White history, of course, tells us that we lost the clash of cultures, and our sometimes shaky sense of identity is further shaken by white condescension or paternalism. I can recall clearly a high school pep rally in the early 1960s prior to a basketball tournament when one of the varsity players likened the team to the United States Cavalry in days gone by. Not only was the team ready, willing, and able he said, it even had two good Indian scouts—the two Indian players on the team. I cannot help but think that a one-sided history contributed to the sense that it was acceptable to make such a statement. And we Indian players and students certainly accepted the analogy without comment or

Joseph Marshall III

protest. We had heard and read the same history. History, after all, is shaped by attitudes and shapes attitudes.

The European and Euro-American of the nineteenth century had a penchant for suspiciously and fearfully regarding anything different as an enemy or a challenge; and enemies and challenges were generally regarded as impediments to civilization. This thinking held true for their Oregon Trail experience. During that chapter of Euro-American history, everything was an obstacle. The land, the rivers, the weather, the climate, and anything closely connected to any of them. Since Indians lived their lives intimately associated with all aspects of the natural environment, it was easy to regard them as another obstacle rather than groups of people with feelings, territories, communities, societies, values, traditions, languages, and histories. And if they were not regarded as obstacles because of their lifestyles, they were regarded as obstacles simply because they were different—since *different* was defined by Euro-Americans as "less than." To think of a group or groups of people as "less than" or "not as good as" oneself or one's own race or society is to dehumanize.

The process of dehumanization is a three-phase cycle. First, this process involves defining a group of people (or an individual) as lacking any semblance of worthiness to, any similarity and any connection whatsoever with what was or is for the moment defined as "civilized," based on emotion and self-serving rationalization. Second, it entails following up with action and/or policy based on the previous definition. Third, it seeks to justify the first two phases with more self-serving rationalization.

History tells us that 350,000 emigrants traveled along the Oregon Trail over a twenty-year period beginning in 1843. How many of them, I wonder, lived in fear of Indians because prevailing opinion was thoroughly negative. The fear of and generally low opinion of Indians was all too frequently not based on firsthand experience, since few of the emigrants actually had personal contact with an Indian or Indians prior to or during the trek along the trail. A significant basis for emigrant fears and negative opinions about Indians was someone else's opinion.

It is difficult to conjecture how far back one would have had to trace this opinion chain to find anyone who actually had had the kind of firsthand contact to form a meaningful basis for any opinion—good or bad. Furthermore, it should be noted that by the early 1840s, the Indian tribes in the eastern part of what was by then the United States had been decimated, nearly decimated, or under some type of rigid white governmental control. Since the white emigrants who traveled the Oregon Trail were from that part of the country, even a cursory awareness of the condition and circumstances of eastern tribes would have been enough of a basis for racially biased opinions about Indians in the West. Therefore, along with hopes and dreams for a new life for themselves, the emigrants also carried a mind-set about Indians that would eventually dash Indian hopes and dreams. It was a mind-set that existed, with few exceptions, throughout white American society—even in the highest echelons of the government.

Joseph Marshall III

In 1831, the Cherokee of Georgia had won a legal battle. *Cherokee Nation v. Georgia* had gone all the way to the United States Supreme Court. It began when the Cherokee learned that the state of Georgia would try to extend state jurisdiction over tribal lands and take the lands to add them to several existing counties. Because the Cherokee had signed a series of eleven treaties ratified and confirmed by the United States Senate, the Supreme Court held that they were entitled not only to seek redress in the federal court system but also stated that they had an unquestionable and unquestioned right to the lands they occupied.

President Andrew Jackson had already signed an Indian Removal Act in 1830 with clear intent to relocate eastern tribes to a specially designated "Indian Territory" west of the Mississippi. The Cherokee's victory in court meant little to Jackson, who at one point challenged the chief justice to enforce the ruling of his court. Under the "legal" auspices of the Indian Removal Act, he ordered the army to remove the Cherokee from their land.

Along with the Cherokee, the Choctaw, Creek, Chickasaw, and Seminole were known as the "Five Civilized Tribes," primarily because some of their people had adopted the ways of the whites, finding a new cultural mix of old tribal ways and progress. Since acquiring Indian land was the main purpose of the Indian Removal Act, such acculturation meant little. All five tribes were included in the presidential removal order.

The Choctaw of Mississippi were the first to go. Several groups of up to a thousand were escorted to

Indian Territory by the United States Army beginning in 1834. About a quarter of them died during the forced migration and more after they reached Oklahoma. In 1836, the Creek of Alabama, fifteen thousand of them, were removed, with about 3,500 dying during and after the removal. The Chickasaw were removed from northern Mississippi, after having been moved there from western Kentucky and Tennessee. Cholera killed many after their arrival in Oklahoma. The Seminole resisted the most tenaciously, forcing United States soldiers and marines to pursue them in the swamps and jungles of Florida. In the end, three thousand of them were removed in the early 1840s. In 1838, the Cherokee suffered the first removal after a protracted campaign against them by the federal government and the state of Georgia. The removals of 1838 to 1839 came to be known as the Trail of Tears. Approximately four thousand Cherokee died during confinement in stockades as they waited to be removed, as well as during the removal itself. Removals during the intense heat of summer and the freezing temperatures of winter along the eight hundred mile route from western Georgia, exacerbated by inadequate food rations and medicines, as well as preying bandits, all took a toll.

Since 1843 has long been held as the year of the first major migrations along the Oregon Trail, many of those travelers more than likely carried with them the knowledge, or at least the feeling, that Indians had no rights that had to be honored by white men. After all, did not a president of the United States clearly demonstrate as much?

Joseph Marshall III

The northern Plains, encompassing an area that is now Nebraska, the Dakotas, and the eastern portions of Wyoming and Montana, were the last stronghold of several nomadic tribes: the Northern Cheyenne, the Northern Arapaho, the Crow, and the Lakota. By the early 1840s there was a definite Euro-American presence at places like Fort Laramie in southeastern Wyoming and the steamboat landing at Fort Pierre on the Missouri River in what is now central South Dakota. Missionaries, trappers, fur traders, and soldiers were well known to the people of the northern Plains. And certainly by then, information regarding the fate of Indians in the eastern part of the country had reached the area. But the most telling portent came in 1837 with smallpox epidemics that killed two thousand Lakota among some of the bands that lived close to the Missouri and all but wiped out the already small tribe of Mandan further to the north. Numbering about two thousand prior to the epidemic, the Mandan were reduced to two hundred or less by that fall and winter. The obvious source of the disease was the whites. It had been carried north along the Missouri River on one of their steamboats. Not surprisingly, then, Euro-Americans were regarded with definite apprehension on one end of the scale and outright fear on the other. A people who could cause the deaths of thousands of Lakota and Mandan without firing a single shot in battle was certainly something to be feared.

For the tribes of the northern Plains in the early 1800s, the prospect of whites coming into their lands and their lives had been a growing threat. So while whites were not totally unknown, the sudden influx of tens of thousands of them along the Oregon Trail was a surprise. It became all too obvious very quickly that whites represented a kind of threat that had never before been faced.

In spite of the apprehension and uneasiness about so many whites moving into and through their territories, Indians were curious about them. Many initial Indian-white contacts were peaceful. If nothing else, representatives of the two groups participated in the basic human interaction of trade. But two stories I heard as a child suggest that there were other positive interactions. They were about two different groups of Lakota warriors, and both were more than likely based on incidents that occurred prior to 1854.

In the first, a group of Lakota warriors was traveling south in what is now northwestern Nebraska. While still north of the Shell (North Platte) River, the warriors encountered a strange sight—a white man's wagon with four strange animals tethered nearby. In the shade of the wagon was a white woman and two small children, alone with no other whites in the immediate area.

The warriors were aware that many whites had been traveling west along the Holy Road through this part of Lakota territory. Therefore, they surmised that these whites were some of those travelers. Toward sundown the warriors approached the woman's camp. She and her children, of course, were utterly terrified by the sudden appearance of mounted Lakota warriors and crawled under the wagon, cowering in wide-eyed fear.

The warriors spoke soothingly to the three whites and even tried hand signs. Finally, at sundown the women and children emerged from beneath the wagon, probably resigned to facing torture and a terrible death. But after one man started a fire, boiled water in a pot, made tea from wild peppermint, and offered a cup of it to the woman, she and the children seemed relieved. One of the warriors discovered a fresh grave, and all of them could only guess that it was the woman's husband. They could only further speculate that she was alone with her children to mourn.

The warriors stayed with the woman and her children for at least two more days. Two of the men hunted and brought back fresh meat, while one or two others helped the children watch the oxen (the four strange animals) as they grazed and watered. The women spoke and pointed toward the river and off to the west. Not knowing what else to do, two warriors went west, returning with news that a large group of whites in wagons like the woman's were traveling to the west. One of the scout warriors drew a picture of wagons in the sand, which elicited an effusive, positive response from the woman.

The warriors talked and decided that the woman and her children would be better off with their own people. The scout warrior drew yet another picture of a lone wagon, far from the others. When he then drew a line from it to the picture of the other wagons, this prompted an emphatic nod from the woman.

The oxen were hitched to the wagon, and the three whites with their escort of Lakota warriors headed west. The oxen were excrutiatingly slow no matter how often the warriors stung them with blows from their riding quirts. But by late the next the day they came in sight of a dust cloud that hung low over the Shell River. It turned out to be a line of wagons.

The warriors kept pushing the oxen until well after sundown. Within sight of hundreds of campfires, they took their leave of the woman and her children. They rode far into the night until they were well away from the night camp of wagons and whites. The next day they continued their trek toward Pawnee country, crossing over the Shell River and the Holy Road as they went.

The second story is similar in nature. According to this story, a group of young warriors had been lying below the crest of hills to the north of the Shell River, watching the last of a long line of wagons moving off toward the west along the Holy Road. That evening as they were riding home, a soft whimpering caught their attention. They followed the sounds and found a small white boy crouched in some shrubs. Either because he was too terrified to act or simply glad to see someone, the boy allowed himself to be taken by the young men. That night they fed him and gave him a place to sleep.

The next day, after deciding that the boy had probably wandered away from one of the wagons they had been watching, the warriors took him west, staying out of sight of the wagon train until they were slightly ahead of it. When the train stopped sometime before sundown, two of the warriors took the boy and sneaked up very close to it. From there they let him go back to his people.

There is an inclination to want to believe such stories because they reveal the positive side of human nature. The old people who told the stories would invariably discuss the pros and cons of the warriors helping the woman and her family or the lost boy. But

Joseph Marshall III

nearly all of them would conclude that they probably would have done the same thing, since those white people were pitiful and needed help. If the warriors in either of these stories were anything like my grandfathers, they certainly would have had the compassion to help. However, there is an unfortunate tendency on the part of many people to dismiss such anecdotes as simply stories without any possible basis in fact—since they fly in the face of beliefs about Indians at the time. Admittedly, I have found little to corroborate these stories in the research I have done of Oregon Trail diaries. Yet I wonder if a recently widowed white woman and a lost and presumably disoriented boy would have been able to convince others that they had been helped by Indians. Perhaps the woman thought better of telling her story. And even if the boy had, who would have believed him? According to prevailing Euro-American opinions of the day, lending assistance to helpless white people was something Indians simply did not do.

As more and more emigrants filled the travel corridor called the Oregon Trail, their presence in overwhelming numbers adversely impacted the lives of the tribes. One of the most immediate consequences was the alteration of habitat and migration patterns of game animals. For people whose daily lives and basic existence were inextricably intertwined with the land, its cycles, and its other inhabitants, the movement of deer, elk, and (especially) bison away from usual ranges and migratory patterns brought unwanted and unwelcome change. The kind of change with an effect not unlike the ripple of a stone tossed into a quiet pond.

The Oregon Trail followed a natural travel corridor first used by large migratory animals and then by the pre-European inhabitants of the region. It was a corridor that had been well known and well used by many species for thousands of years before it figured prominently in Euro-American history. The sudden, heavy human traffic along the corridor first impacted four-legged species. Hunting pressure exerted by the emigrants was a factor, but not one as great as their mere presence in such large numbers. The result was that the four-leggeds stayed away from the area, and the nomadic hunting tribes that depended on them had to move into different hunting territories. Even if such forays were into the territories of friendly tribes, there was nonetheless some strain on friendly relations. And going into the territories of enemy tribes was an outright invitation to war.

Of course, the emigrants traveling the trail in pursuit of their dreams and on their way to building a nation were ignorant of the effects they were having on the land and all the inhabitants already there. Even if they had known, given the attitudes fostered by the treatment of Indians in the East, nothing would have happened any differently. The phenomenon of the Oregon Trail was overwhelming for the Euro-Americans, too. Had there been a question raised concerning the impact of their presence on the prior human inhabitants of the regions through which they traveled, it would have been a whisper in the midst of a gale. A compelling truth is that among the diaries kept by a number of the emigrants, there was no voice that raised a genuine concern for Indian welfare to the point that it altered the course of the trail or history. Furthermore, stories handed down through the mechanism of Indian oral tradition about the impact of white emigration were not available to non-Indians, thereby underscoring the sense that there was only one side to the history being made.

The most obvious fact about the Euro-Americans traveling along the trail was their sheer numbers. Next was their technology, especially with regard to weaponry. But the two factors that caused the most havoc and devastation for Indian people were not as visible. One was attitude, and the other was disease.

Indians who had no choice but to contend firsthand with the travelers along the Oregon Trail were well aware that whites were the source of strange and terrible sicknesses. In 1849, that fear was borne out by a cholera outbreak among the Pawnee, Kiowa, and Lakota. For the Kiowa it was the second costly epidemic they had endured in nine years, having suffered an onslaught of smallpox before. The Pawnee lost roughly half of their people, and many of the survivors were so spiritually devastated that they refused to bury those who had died from cholera. To the north the Lakota were somewhat less affected, but only numerically, and the experience only served to deepen mistrust of whites and their motives. Some Lakota thought that the illness had been deliberately brought among them.

After the initial migrations and the sense of uneasiness grew on both sides, the white emigrants became increasingly concerned for their physical safety. The same sentiment existed among the tribes, but for different reasons. Of course, the emigrants probably did not consider that they had done anything to adversely affect their own well-being. On the other hand, after hundreds of thousands of head of bison (perhaps millions) began staying away from the region of the trail on both sides of it; after the Shell River itself was polluted with the excrement and urine from thousands of head of emigrant livestock, refuse, and animal carcasses; after graves began to pock the land on either side of the travel route; after hundreds and thousands of items of household and personal belongings of various sizes and shapes were errantly discarded to rot where they lay, the tribes knew they were facing not only a direct and immediate threat to their safety and well-being, but a very real threat to their long-term futures. What exactly to do about the situation was a source of ongoing debate.

While older leaders debated, younger men talked of war parties against the wagon trains. Though concensus among the older leaders was in general agreement with the younger warriors—that attacking the wagon trains was the most immediate and best way to stop them—there were two factors that prevented all-out war along the Oregon Trail. First, the warriors of many tribes knew that the emigrants were far better armed. But the second factor was far more compelling: the threat of coming into contact with disease. That fear was real enough to stop many warriors from attacking, sometimes at the last possible moment.

The number of actual Indian attacks during the twenty-year migration will never be known. But of the approximately thirty-five thousand emigrants who

84

died from various causes during that time (according to many current extrapolations from data in emigrant diaries), I suspect that less than one thousand died as a direct result of Indian attack. Perhaps, less than five hundred. In the final analysis, cholera and smallpox were far more powerful allies for the emigrants than they themselves probably realized.

In any event, the uneasiness of the emigrants was part of the reason for the 1851 treaty gathering at Fort Laramie and the only reason for the second Lakota name given to the Oregon Trail. Some of the stories I have heard about the trail prior to 1851 made reference to *Wasicu Tacunku kin*—the White Man's Road. After the 1851 gathering of tribes at Fort Laramie, Wyoming, which resulted in the Fort Laramie Treaty of 1851, the trail became known as the Holy Road to the Lakota. However, the name had nothing to do with anything spiritual, moral, or just on the part of those who traveled it.

The Fort Laramie Treaty of 1851 is remembered by the Lakota, Dakota, Cheyenne, Crow, Mandan, Blackfeet, Hidatsa, Arikara, and Arapaho for three things, which were the basic terms of the treaty. First, it was the first time they had encountered the concept of artificial boundaries drawn on a map. Second, the peace commissioners representing the United States of America presumed to tell enemy tribes to stop fighting with one another forever. Third, they told the tribes to stop harassing the white emigrants traveling along the White Man's Road.

To the Lakota, generally speaking, the 1851 Fort Laramie Treaty was somewhat ludicrous. Where, they wondered, did the whites get the power to say where the land should begin and end simply by drawing lines on a map? Where did they get the power to tell anyone to suddenly stop being who and what they were? And how, they wondered, could a group of people be under the protection of a "Great Father" who was so far away that he could not see his people on the road they must stay on to be protected by him? Perhaps, came the suggestion, the road is sacred or holy in some fashion. Thereafter, the White Man's Road, known in other circles as the Oregon Trail, the Mormon Trail, and the Platte River Road, became known to the Lakota as "the Holy Road."

The accidental arrival of Columbus was the beginning of terrible, unwanted change for the indigenous inhabitants of the continent he stumbled upon. There are several chapters to this difficult story. One of the most difficult, especially for the Lakota, is the Holy Road/Oregon Trail.

For the Euro-Americans the Oregon Trail might have represented a character-forging test of courage and tenacity, it might well have been a pathway for individual hopes and dreams, and it might have been a time that helped build a new nation. On the other hand, it was no less a test of character, courage, and tenacity for those who saw their lands rent in two and their futures swept away by the flood of people who regarded themselves as better than anything that was on, in, and above the land.

If some saw their dreams take shape and grow, others saw theirs fade and die with each cut of an iron-rimmed wagon wheel into the beloved earth. If in the

Joseph Marshall III

end one nation was born, many nations suffered and some died as a consequence of that birthing. Some of those nations were the Missouri, Iowa, Kansa, Osage, Oto, Omaha, Pawnee, Ponca, Kiowa, Arapaho, Cheyenne, Sioux, Eastern Shoshoni, Crow, Bannock, Northern Paiute, Cayuse, Nez Perce, Wallawalla, Umatilla, Molala, Tenino, Wishram, Palouse, Yakima, and Western Shoshoni. These peoples lived on or near the region of the Oregon Trail. But in the final anyalysis every pre-European nation was affected by it and other events, which are sometimes, in some circles, still regarded as the more important aspects of human history on this continent.

The old ones that I knew in my youth spoke of the Holy Road in quiet, hushed voices—if they spoke at all about it. They were not awed by the Oregon Trail; but they were awed by the patriotic efforts of grandparents and great-grandparents who, during the time of the Holy Road, met and faced the inexorable push of unwanted change with wisdom and fortitude. Now and then, one of them would glance my way and say, "We should not forget the Holy Road, and we should not let it happen again."

The sesquicentennial of the Oregon Trail was in 1993. There was at least one symbolic reenactment that I know of. A man from Wyoming drove some wagons, drawn by horses, from Missouri to Oregon. And there were observations and celebrations of the sesquicentennial in communities and states along the route. But as far as I know, none was conducted by Indian tribes or groups, That should speak volumes regarding Indian opinion of a chapter in American history regarded largely by many non-Indian Americans as a positive aspect of the "opening up" and "settlement" of the West. There is a single and clear message here: What is a reason to celebrate for one group of people may be a reason for somber reflection by another, or even a reason to mourn.

Richard Williams, a Lakota and Cheyenne educator, is intensely interested in the history of both of his ancestral tribes. Commenting for a newspaper article (published in 1993 in the Casper Star-Tribune, Casper, Wyoming), he stated that "Indians celebrating the Oregon Trail would be like the Jews celebrating the Holocaust." Further, he is quick to point out that the tribes who signed the 1851 Fort Laramie Treaty agreed to allow the white emigrants to use the Oregon Trail (Holy Road) only as an access route to their final destinations further to the west. "But they [the emigrants] were like a river that eventually flooded the land instead of simply flowing through it. And it was the start of the demise of the Indian ways of life."

Norman Wilson, a Rosebud Sioux and a past president of the Rosebud Sioux Tribal Council, indicated that there was virtually no publicity about the trail on the Rosebud Sioux Indian Reservation in the summer of 1993. To him, that was just as well. "It [the Oregon Trail] is really nothing to celebrate," he said.

Jerry Aday, a Cherokee and Executive Director of the Mid-America All Indian Center in Wichita, Kansas, reported that no information or publicity about the Oregon Trail sesquicentennial had crossed his desk in 1993. Nor was he personally aware of any tribes in the area celebrating it. Wichita has a Native

Joseph Marshall III

American population of about five thousand, representing some seventy-seven tribes.

But though Indian tribes may not have celebrated the Oregon Trail sesquicentennial, a few chose to look at the anniversary date as a unique opportunity. Mardell Plainfeather, a member of the Crow Tribe of Montana who works for the National Park Service, compares the Euro-American migration along the Oregon Trail to the Battle of the Little Bighorn. Both were ultimately sad and tragic events for Indians. "But," she said, "the...observance and celebration of the Oregon Trail is an opportunity for us [Indians] to tell our side."

For twenty years beginning in 1843, hundreds of thousands of white emigrants made the trek along the Oregon Trail with the attitude that the lands through which they traveled were empty and there for the taking. One hopes that the same kind of attitude did not prevail during the observation of the sesquicentennial and does not happen anytime the human history of this continent is told.

There is always more than one side to any story. History, therefore, should not be the domain of those who consider themselves the "winners" to the exclusion of those who are perceived to be the "losers," any more than the Plains (and all of the western lands) should have been considered empty and uninhabited.

From one end of this continent to the other, the interaction of two cultures vastly different from one another was basically one of acculturation, conflict, and assimilation. We too often overlook or ignore that it was *human* interaction predicated, guided, and given substance by human vices and virtues, by human strengths and weaknesses, and by the worst and the best of human nature.

I return to the vicinity of my boyhood as often as I can. It is part of the ancestral territory of my tribe, the Sicangu Lakota, before it became the Rosebud Sioux Reservation and we became known as the Rosebud Sioux Tribe. On that land I feel most strongly connected to that part of me which is Sicangu Lakota. That sense of connection comes through my grandparents. Their wisdom, their humor, their love, their humanity—everything they were and are so easily transcends the span of years whenever I stand on their land. It is during such moments that I come closest to understanding how it must have felt to be separated from the core of individual and tribal identity. The land.

Since I had come to know the land following in my grandfather's footsteps, I can easily imagine that it was the same for some other Lakota boy three or four generations before. Or a Cheyenne, Arapaho, Kiowa, or Pawnee.

I imagine it is the 1860s or 1870s on the Plains and an old Indian man is providing yet another lesson about hunting for his grandson: They are riding to a favorite spot, a tree-sheltered meadow along a small stream where the deer were always certain to be. A place where the old man has hunted many times. A place where his father and grandfather had taken him. But on this day they find a strange, four-cornered dwelling made from small slabs of earth standing in the meadow. And the deer are gone, and the land is different. The old man has no explanation for the

Joseph Marshall III

sudden change, and there is no choice but to find other places to hunt with his grandson.

However, there came a day when there were no more places to hunt because the land was filled with strange people. People who were changing the land, and in turn changing the people who were once part of the land. In time, the boy knew the land was different because he saw it in his grandfather. Because his grandfather no longer knew the land.

Although I never shared this product of my imagination with either of my grandparents, one day my grandfather did talk about changes in the land. Even though he pointed out that the land does change, he quietly insisted that though the appearance of the land might change, its spirit never will—especially if those who were here before remember that the land is part of who and what they are.

I often feel the truth of this statement. At any given moment anywhere, I can reach into my memories and see, hear, and feel my grandparents. I can hear their voices, see their smiles, and even now hang my head as I recall a quiet admonition. But when I stand on their land, I can see, hear, and feel them so much more intensely. I can see my grandmother enjoying the cooling caress of a gentle evening breeze after a hot summer day, or see her dig a wild turnip out of the earth and add it to her cache. I can hear her humming an old song in time with her rhythmic pounding as she smashes freshly picked chokecherries with a hammerstone. I can see my grandfather part the blades of a thick clump of grass to reveal the speckled eggs in a meadowlark's nest, and then hear him quietly remind me that we should disturb it no further.

An Indian Viewpoint of History

And yet there is something more than that familial connection to the land. Something larger and older, because that connection includes all who have lived on, in, above, and with the land. One generation collectively enables the many different forms of the next, as each form specifically reproduces itself. And each generation returns to the land and becomes memories and, eventually, sustenance for subsequent generations. To feel a connection to the land is to feel all others who are and were connected to it.

I have seen many landscapes—tropical jungles, deserts, tundra, mountains, and seashores. There is beauty and vitality in all of those places. But there is nothing that touches the ancient part of my spirit the way the prairies do. It is these wide-open expanses that beckon the wanderer in me and affirm my grandfather's reality; the land is part of who and what I am.

Given that reality, I can almost understand how the Oregon Trail must have emotionally and spiritually affected those Pawnee, Arapaho, Cheyenne, Lakota, and so on, who were watching a part of themselves changing perceptibly with each turn of a wagon wheel. Fortunately, there were some who remembered that the land was part of who and what they were. And if the land could endure change—and in some instances overcome it—so could they. Given this, perhaps, the Holy Road will never happen again.

This was a land of many diverse human cultures prior to 1492. It still is—culturally, ethnically, politically, racially, attitudinally, economically, and spiritually. That is the contemporary reflection from

Joseph Marshall III

the landscape of our history. It is a heritage that belongs to all of us. There are moments, however, when I wonder what the landscape would be like if we—the Indians—would have persevered in the West. What would the geography be? Would there be less or more of an acrimonious relationship with the United States government if there was a corridor of independent nations in the middle of the West? What would the demographics reflect? Would there be air and water pollution and the decimation of entire forests? What would life be like for Euro-Americans and Native Americans alike had the terms of the 1851 Fort Laramie Treaty been honored, and the emigrants had only passed *through* the land? Would we have been able to reclaim it and heal it, or would the devastation from the migration of 350,000 people and the slices from thousands of their wagon wheels have been a mortal wound in any case?

Speculation and dreams aside, it is time to look at our history honestly, accept the reality of it, and then pass it on to the coming generations with all of its wonder, mundaneness, heroism, brutality, and humanity. And not once must we forget that it is a story of human interaction with many stories within it. We cannot change anything of it, but we can use it to shape tomorrow for our descendants. We owe it to them to learn all the tough lessons history can teach us. We owe it to them to remember the way we have come, so tomorrow they will not lose their way, or forget, or alter, or obliterate, or ignore the trails we are leaving.

Indian Art

It is a fact that many misconceptions exist with regard to things Indian, or Native American. One of these misconceptions is that Indian art has always been a separate discipline within the structure of Indian cultures. The truth is that utilitarian and decorative crafts were a necessary part of physical and spiritual existence for native peoples on this continent. For example, the woman who made a willow basket did not consider herself an artist or an artisan. She saw herself as contributing to the survival and comfort of her family with the ability to make that basket as a container for foods and other items. The man who carved and baked a shale pipe bowl and fashioned a wooden stem for it did not consider his effort art, but as something that enabled him and others to acknowledge the communion of Earth and all who lived on it. Clearly, while baskets and pipes are being made today, the motivation is not purely utilitarian or spiritual. It is to meet a demand for things Indian. A demand from non-Indians is primarily responsible for "Indian art" as we know it today and has prompted us to apply the term

94

"art" retrospectively to traditional forms of expression. For example, pictographs and petroglyphs which were probably intended as family or tribal records of events are now called "rock art."

Indian art certainly is a separate and identifiable aspect of contemporary Indian cultures because the creative and expressive nature of Indian people has responded to the demand. But while there is an apparent identity, the source of "Indian art" does not always reflect the Indian and is not always under Indian control.

A few years ago a non-Indian shopkeeper pointed out to me a replication of a Plains Indian cultural artifact and declared that it was "authentically Indian," because his son—who had made the artifact—had been "adopted" into a Plains tribe. In other instances there is no such pretext. Non-Indians produce two- or three-dimensional art and unabashedly declare it "authentically Indian," based on the fact that the piece or work resembles something that an Indian did or would have done. And now and then some "artisan" will proudly announce that his or her work is better than an Indian ever did or could do, In somewhat the same vein, a non-Indian acquaintance of mine recently questioned the authenticity of Lakota arrows I had made because they "looked different" from some he had seen in an old photograph. It seems to me that these instances point to a basic confusion regarding the highly visible medium and increasingly popular and lucrative business of Indian art. What is authentic Indian art and who should decide what it is or is not?

As an artisan who handcrafts traditional Lakota weapons (such as bows and arrows, lances, and so forth) and as one who enjoys Indian art, as well as a

Native American who is sensitive to the dilution of Native American cultures from contact with non-Indian influences, I feel strongly that Indian art is an aspect of Indian culture and identity that should be defined by the Indian (or Native American) community.

As a Lakota speaker I do not know a Lakota word for art. There are, of course, words (in Lakota) for quill, paint, sketch, carve, sew, and to make. Within pre-European cultures, all of those kinds of activities and skills were part of life. They were necessary because most pre-European cultures depended on the individual's initiative, creativity, and crafting skills to produce artifacts that were necessary to ensure survival and comfort for all, as well as to help preserve tradition and history through the generations.

In pre-European tribal cultures each person learned a variety of skills peculiar to his or her societal role. Males learned to make weapons and tools for hunting and fishing, for example, and females learned to make household items such as rawhide storage cases or baskets. In some cultures there were specialty skills, such as carving ceremonial masks, sandpainting, totem carving, or wintercount drawing. But even those skills were regarded as being within the parameters of necessity. Although some individuals excelled with one skill or another and produced quillwork or scrimshaw or baskets or bows that were either far more aesthetically pleasing or functioned much better than most, such skilled individuals were not considered *artists*. They were, of course, considered to be superior at making baskets or bows or producing a certain design. Although, some individuals—both male and female—

Joseph Marshall III

became well known for having an exceptional skill or the ability to produce a high-quality product, most such individuals did not actively leverage that skill or product into material gain, Therefore, if the concept of "artist" did not exist, neither did the concept of "art."

The concept of "Indian art" came into existence when someone saw and expressed an interest in an intricately or beautifully made artifact, such as quilled or beaded moccasins, an effigy carved from walrus tusk, a woven willow basket, or a totem pole, and took steps to acquire it. Or perhaps when someone like Geronimo made and sold bows and arrows after he had been captured.

If art is the product of human creativity, effort, and skill, it follows then that Indian art is the product of Indian creativity, effort, and skill. But it is absolutely necessary to define what "Indian" means or encompasses so that we can understand the depth and breadth of this relatively new phenomenon.

Indian (like Native American and American Indian) is the generic label used in reference to two million people who are members of the several hundred surviving tribes descended from the pre-European, indigenous inhabitants of this continent. This is an ethnological definition not to be confused with the political definition in the United States based on "federal recognition."

Federal recognition is what the phrase implies. Political recognition of an Indian tribe by the United States government, often through the instrument of a treaty or the establishment of a reservation. Federal recognition means eligibility for delivery of services and/or funding from the federal government in return for having given up land. All of the United States was at one time Indian-controlled territory, but the current combined landholdings of the approximately five hundred "federally recognized" tribes or nations is comparable to the size of the state of Minnesota. There are many ethnologically identifiable tribes without federal recognition, and many who have had federal recognition rescinded (largely due to loss of land base) by the federal government.

It is my opinion that the term "Indian art" is really only a semantic veneer and that the heart, soul, and spirit of it emanates from many separate and independent parts. There are probably about four hundred distinct, ethnically identifiable (as opposed to "federally recognized") tribes or nations left in the United States. Each of those tribes or nations has its own name rooted in its own language, although many are now primarily known by "Europeanized" versions of other tribal words or names—such as *Sioux* for the Lakota, Dakota, and Nakota; *Navaho* or *Navajo* for the Diné; *Cherokee* for the Tsalagi; *Arapaho* for Nanahe, and so on. Therefore, the old adage "there is more than meets the eye" is especially applicable here.

Pre- and post-contact tribes on this continent had and have separate and distinct ethnic identities, languages, values, traditions, customs, and all other traits within the parameters of culture. Therefore, beyond the generic label of "Indian art" is Seminole art, Choctaw art, Duwamish art, Hopi art, and so on, hundreds of times over. The term "Indian art" will not diminish in use, and it obviously does serve as a

Joseph Marshall III

general identifier. But the perception of what Indian art is should not be obscured by such a generic and amalgamative label.

Indian art, then, is not a style. It is a multitribal, multicultural, and multidimensional form of expression that comes from the totality of prehistorical, historical, and contemporary Indian experience. Whatever its origins, it is empowered and sustained by its individual, tribal, and pan-Indian identities and must remain connected to itself to remain Indian art.

Indian art does not need to be so esoteric as to be narrow, but there does need to be a certain degree of exclusivity where the practioners—artists, artisans, and craftspeople—are concerned. This leads us back to the production of "authentic" Indian art by non-Indians. That, in the strictest and fairest definition, cannot happen.

Whether it is two-dimensional or three-dimensional, the creation of a product that depicts or is a medium of Indian expression or a representation of a specific tribal/cultural artifact is only authentically Indian if the artist, artisan, or craftsperson is a recognized member of an ethnically and/or legally identified Indian tribe or nation. This does not, however, prevent non-Indians from producing anything which represents or resembles Indian art in any form.

Indian artists, artisans, and craftspeople produce works that depict many facets of many Indian tribal cultures. They paint, sculpt, bead, quill, carve, sew, sketch, weave, dye, scrape, braid, knap, bend, and pound. Kachina dolls, pottery, squash blossoms, beaded moccasins, totems, dugout canoes, drums, medallions, bows and arrows, hair ties, and earrings (to list but a few) provide a visible, tangible insight into and connection to an era, a place, a people, and even a certain individual.

The Indian person whose skill and knowledge produces a drum, for example, is the medium for that insight and connection; and that skill and knowledge came by way of a learning process inspired more than likely by a broad racial heritage and a specific tribal bloodline—not to mention a love of beauty, a desire to create, and the need to make a dollar or two. Except for heritage and bloodline, the non-Indian who imitates Indian art can know and appreciate the process, but non-Indians can merely replicate. Only Indians can produce Indian art.

Today, Indian art is a lucrative business. Many shops throughout the country routinely stock "Indian" items, from paintings to arrowheads. Unfortunately, a certain percentage of those items are not produced by Indians, and there are retailers who do not care. As long as an item is remotely Indian in appearance, it is labeled "Indian," and often the buyers of such products are unaware that the authenticity of their purchases may be questionable. The object itself may be incorrect as to design, configuration, colors, and materials; and the artist or artisan may not be the correct race or nationality. (I recently saw poorly made "authentic Cree Indian artifacts" at a crafts fair in Sweden, made by an Italian claiming Cree Indian blood.) Not only are the buyers in such instances perpetuating the production of fakes, they are cheating themselves out of owning something authentically Indian-made as well as denying an economic benefit to Indians who do produce art in many forms.

Joseph Marshall III

It would be immensely logical and fair for non-Indian artists, artisans, and craftspeople who have a genuine love and respect for Indian culture and art to let it be known that their own products are the work of non-Indians. I know that some do; but I also know that some do not, motivated either by the lure, of higher profit or the satisfaction of duping an unsuspecting buyer or collectors. Similarly, stores that buy and sell Indian art should be certain of their sources and label and price their merchandise accordingly. Some do, and some even buy only from Indian artists, artisans, and craftspeople. But there are others who buy and sell any artifact with a bead and a feather or a wavy line on a piece of pottery as "authentically Indian," whether it is or not.

Of course, a large part of the responsibility for maintaining the integrity of Indian art and the integrity of the Indian art business rests with the Indian community, squarely on the shoulders of those of us who are artists, artisans, and craftspeople, as well as Indian wholesalers and retailers. There are organizations like the Indian Arts and Crafts Association (based in Albuquerque, New Mexico) that can and do help.

One area of Indian art that is particularly vulnerable to misrepresentation or false advertising is the production of traditional cultural artifacts. The high demand for objects such as Iroquois false face masks, Cheyenne feather bonnets, Eskimo dance masks, Algonquin birch bark baskets, Acoma Pueblo pottery, Osage cradle boards, Crow hair pipe breastplates, Pima calendar sticks, and so forth, has apparently forced wholesalers and retailers to provide those items from non-Indian craftspeople. Another aspect that is ignored by a rush to meet demand is cultural/tribal authenticity. Is an object which is said to be an Eskimo dance mask really an Eskimo dance mask or the best imitation that money can buy? This type of authenticity must be based on two factors: first, the artisan and second, the adherence to basic culturally/tribally specific designs, raw materials, colors, and crafting techniques.

We should expect the same of those artists who desire to depict historical or cultural realism in paintings, drawings, sketches, sculptures, and carvings. While it is true that anything produced by an Indian artist or craftsperson is technically "authentically Indian," there must also be cultural and historical accuracy, as well as quality. Unfortunately, I have seen too many cultural or ethnographic artifacts that were not only of questionable quality and workmanship but also far from being culturally and historically accurate. This practice diminishes Indian art and its integrity for everyone from practitioner to retailer to buyer and collectors. If such practices continue, we may end up with yet another aspect of Indian history and culture that is skewed by greed and distorted by ignorance and, arrogance to the point that we eventually forget the true and ancient origins. It is to a certain extent understandable when non-Indians intentionally or unintentionally alter various aspects of Indian history and culture, but that does not mean we should do it to ourselves. We may make money and gain momentary fame, but we are irrevocably altering and even destroying a part of our own culture, thus denying it to our descendants.

Joseph Marshall III

The best way to achieve and maintain cultural and historical accuracy is to rely on firsthand knowledge. If you want to build a cedar flute, for example, then learn the skill from someone who makes and plays cedar flutes; someone who has knowledge beyond the physical process of crafting; someone who can tell you about the spirit and purpose of the flute and how it was woven into the fabric of culture. For your art to have meaning, you must know not only the *how* but the *why*. Then, what you craft becomes more than a mere object. It becomes a tangible connection to a time, a culture, and a people. With the aid of your skill and ancient knowledge, something of the past will touch the minds and the hearts of contemporary people and offer its stories and its spirit. By contrast, if you are only interested in slapping on beads and tying on feathers to make a quick buck, you will never know the real satisfaction of preserving something honest and real.

A secondary resource for information on Indian history and culture is firsthand non-Indian observation recorded in journals and artworks. It is essential to keep in mind, however, that the degree of objectivity of such material, especially journal entries and notations accompanying artwork, was influenced by the preconceived notions and racially biased attitudes on the part of the observer. Therefore, you should take information from such sources with a grain of salt and remember that your basic purpose is to seek knowledge regarding shape, design, color, uses, raw materials, and crafting methods and not to study the editorial comments of the observer. My favorite

sources of this type are George Catlin and Karl
Bodmer, since my particular interest is bows and
arrows as well as the weaponry of the Plains tribes in
general. Catlin and Bodmer provide excellent visual
references through their sketches and paintings as do
(to a lesser degree) Frederic Remington and Charles
Russell at a later period.

Whatever the source of information about
artifacts for the Indian artist, artisan, and craftsperson,
a constant goal should be to remain true to the origins
of a particular artifact and the true history of a specific
time to be portrayed. Unfortunately, this does not
always happen. I recall seeing an advertisement in a
"western history" magazine of a painting that depicted
a scene regarded in some artistic and historical circles
as typical of Plains Indian life. The focus of
the painting was an Indian warrior riding through an
encampment astride his horse. He was, of course,
wearing a "war" bonnet, which is popularly
regarded as something of an omnipresent and
required accoutrement for all male Indians of
the Plains. However, the depiction of the warrior in
the painting was that of a young man who was
obviously neither old nor experienced enough to have
earned the number of eagle feathers in the bonnet.
Except in the case of rare individuals such as the
Oglala Lakota Crazy Horse, a man did not earn
enough eagle feathers to have a bonnet made until at
least the middle of his years as an active warrior.

Another questionable representation in the
painting was the iron bit and the beaded headstall
worn by the horse. Such an occurrence would have

been the exception rather than the rule, since Plains Indian horsemen generally used a single braided rope rein which was placed in the horse's mouth and tied around the jaw. Many Plains tribes trained their horses to respond to cues from hand, knee, leg, and foot pressure and to the rider's weight shifts and therefore did not rely primarily on an iron bit and double reins. Rather than adhering to historical fact, the painter who created this artwork, whether Indian or not, was depicting his or her own concept of "typical" Plains Indian life. While such practice may be within the purview of artistic freedom, such a painting provides a distorted image to any viewer and prospective buyer and, in my opinion, is no better than many motion pictures (such as *They Died with Their Boots On*, the original *Last of the Mohicans*, and just about every John Wayne western), which grossly misrepresent Indian history, life, and culture. With the benefit of better research and, perhaps, less inclination to guess at or invent Indian culture, this painter could easily have produced an accurate representation of a fascinating era in Plains Indian life.

If the artist who produced the painting discussed above is non-Indian, then it is not Indian art. It is art with an Indian theme. Even if it were historically and culturally accurate, it would still be art about Indians and not by an Indian. Because such a definition of Indian art is very broad, it may be useful to divide Indian art into two period categories in relation to the contemporary art world: works that focus on pre-reservation cultures and works produced since the inception of reservations. The rationale for the latter category is the introduction of new materials.

Indian Art

Euro-American materials used in the production of Indian art were more readily and abundantly available beginning with the inception of reservations. Materials such as canvas, cloth thread, pencils, commercially manufactured paintbrushes, paints, various weaves of cloth, and paper, for example. Notable exceptions are glass beads and trade cloth, which were used specifically by Europeans and Euro-Americans as trade items long before reservations.

The availability of Euro-American materials did not, in and of themselves, drastically change the form and identity of what we now label Indian art so much as they provided interesting mediums for expression of traditional forms: quillwork on belt buckles, leather vests, and bracelets; beadwork on watchbands, checkbooks, baseball caps, and cases for pens and cigarette lighters. Characteristically, Indian artists and craftspeople have made the best possible use of mediums and materials available. So while quilled belt buckles and beaded cigarette lighter cases are fine examples of the application of traditional methods and materials to commonly used modern cultural items, the process itself is a natural part of change and evolution.

Like any human endeavor, Indian art is ever changing and evolving. Some changes have come about through the use of new materials. Other changes have occurred because certain societal roles and values have changed.

One of the less obvious but most notable changes has been traditional gender roles in Plains quilling and beadwork. There was a time when quilling was the

Joseph Marshall III

exclusive domain of females. They did everything from plucking, cleaning, soaking, and dying to braiding and pleating. After European glass beads became popular and largely replaced quills (because there was no preparation time required), quilling still remained a female enterprise. The only exception—if it can be truthfully regarded as such—was in the case of a male who assumed the societal role of a woman.

Today, beadwork and quilling is done by both men and women. Such a change in one aspect of an Indian culture is accepted generally because of the overall societal changes experienced by Indians, especially since the inception of reservations. A shift of gender roles in the production of certain forms of arts and crafts is certainly far more acceptable than the demise of such creative forms as quilling and beadwork. Furthermore, such changes have not lowered aesthetic quality.

Another significant change in Indian art is that skills once considered strictly utilitarian are now regarded as artistic endeavors. One example is the making of traditional clothing and weapons. A forced change in lifestyle rendered these skills obsolete, since after contact with Euro-Americans clothing could be purchased or made out of cloth. Similarly, government annuities and reservations forced the hunter/warrior to focus on farming, thereby eliminating the activity of making weapons for hunting and warfare. The consequence is that those people who can make traditional clothing and bows and arrows are thought to be practitioners of a lost *art*. Even though such activities were not considered art to begin with, they are now regarded as art simply because very few people have specific knowledge and skills with which to produce traditional clothing and weapons. Ironically, in pre-reservation days everyone was expected to have the ability to craft their own weapons and clothing. Change is the father of strange twists, if not art forms. Although many changes have occurred with regard to defining and labeling the utilitarian and decorative crafts that we now call Indian art, as long as Indian artists and craftspeople strive to remember and honor the ancient origins, "Indian art" will maintain its unique identity and its power to change those who make it or come into contact with it. As testimony to this, consider the powerful effect ancient petroglyphs still have on those who witness them today, along with other early forms of Indian expression.

Eleven thousand years ago in a cave somewhere in the Southwest, an ancient hunter took a hard, sharp point of a deer antler and a hammerstone and chipped the story of his successful deer hunt onto the walls of his cave home. He depicted himself as he stalked the deer with atlatl in hand, as he launched the long, stone-pointed shaft, as he butchered the animal, and finally, as he ate the meat. With his creativity and his tools he immortalized himself with the pictures he carved into sandstone. He immortalized an episode out of his existence and perpetuated a part of his world and his time for us to glimpse. Those of us who have seen his art have marvelled at it, and we have made a connection with him, realizing that we share this Earth with someone who lived millenniums ago.

One hundred nineteen years ago, a young Northern Cheyenne warrior by the name of Little

Finger Nail carried a small ledger book with him as he and his people fled northward from confinement in Indian Territory in Oklahoma. He chronicled that flight toward home and freedom with drawings he made in the ledger book.

After unimaginable hardship the Cheyenne made it as far as northern Nebraska. There they split into two groups, hoping to ward off pursuit. Little Finger Nail was with the group that was eventually captured and taken to Fort Robinson, Nebraska. Threatened with cold and starvation in the middle of winter, the captives made a break for freedom. Some of them were killed immediately and some later as the United States Army hunted them down in the snow-covered hills around Fort Robinson. Little Finger Nail was killed protecting a woman and a child. A bullet hole in his ledger book of pictures is testimony to his vision and his sacrifice. Those pictures not only provide a stark, visual account of a tragic period in Northern Cheyenne history, but they also offer a uniquely Indian viewpoint. Such is the gift of Little Finger Nail's art.

In these examples, an ancient hunter and a Cheyenne warrior, with the power of their creativity and expression, reach to us across the barrier of time. They offer us the opportunity to lay aside the burden of our existence by briefly assuming the mantle of theirs.

It is the nature of art that it has the power to transcend many limits and boundaries. It can focus anywhere in the past, present, and future. The only limits are the artist's knowledge, skill, imagination, and desire. An artist may paint, sketch, sculpt, carve wood, make quilts, jewelry, cultural artifacts, dolls, blankets and rugs, woodcuts or sandpaintings. No matter what a particular talent is and no matter how it is expressed and revealed to the world, it has a special power. That power can manifest itself in beauty, in stark reality, in one color or a multitude of colors, and in any shape or form. But most importantly, that power can cause people to gasp in awe, pause in quiet reflection, or perceive an extraordinary dimension of something ordinary. It can transcend the limits of ignorance or personal prejudice and touch the human heart and mind. It can teach, motivate, inspire, revile, ridicule, honor, memorialize, or entertain. It can carry us from reality to fantasy and anywhere in between. And it can be quietly and intensely personal and humbling.

Likewise, each Indian artist, artisan, and craftsperson—with the product of his or her talent—has the potential to cross boundaries and affect people. We can demonstrate to other segments of our society that it is possible to transcend the most rigid barriers of all—those that are built in the human heart and the human mind. Through our art, we can prove that the barriers of opinion, attitude, and prejudice are not strong enough to forever resist the quiet persistence of sincere communication. Art is one significant way to communicate; and communication is the ultimate catalyst for change in any human society.

Indian art—within the context of its many specific tribal identities—is but one aspect of culture. But like language it offers one of the more direct glimpses into the totality of culture. Like language it is intimately connected to every part of culture. And if we remember and preserve our cultures as they once

Joseph Marshall III

were, as much as possible, then we can provide a glimpse of truth as well as beauty to anyone who sees our art.

There will always be the charlatans who will hawk their "authentic" Indian art, be it painting, pottery, or artifacts. The wanna-bes, too, will continue to sell to the unsuspecting their "authentic" works of Indian art, because they were "adopted" into an Indian tribe and learned the ancient secrets of Navajo war bonnets and Sioux squash blossoms. There will always be the obtuse pronouncements from the "experts" about what Indian art is or is not, about how and who should decide who is an Indian artist and who is not. Of course, the federal government will wade in with its bureaucratic omnipotence, flapping its banner of "federal recognition" as the "answer" to every difficulty facing Indians—and generally becoming part of the difficulty rather than helping to alleviate it.

The best antidote to such inauthenticity and exploitation is knowledge and awareness. Only Indians can produce authentic Indian artwork and cultural artifacts. Only Indians can and should decide who is an Indian artist and who is not. Furthermore, we should never forget that two values common to all Indian cultures are truth and honor. For the sake of anyone who genuinely cares about Indian art as well as for the generations of our descendants yet to come, truth and honor should have prominent roles in the production, collection, ownership, and teaching of Indian art.

Two Left Moccasins:
I Become a Member of the Cinema Tribe

I joined the Cinema Tribe in 1993. All I had to do was work with the actor Jon Voight, learn some dialogue in Cheyenne, and wear two left moccasins.

My agent told me later that an initial reaction when I showed up to audition for a (very) minor role in the television movie *Return to Lonesome Dove* was that I looked "too robust." The part I was trying to get was that of a Cheyenne warrior, a leader of a poor, ragtag group of Cheyenne living somewhere in Indian Territory (Oklahoma or thereabouts) sometime after 1876. My first thought was that I probably didn't look poor and ragtag enough. At six feet four and two hundred pounds, I'm used to various reactions to my size. Then I realized that someone was probably trying to politely say that I was overweight for the part.

After the audition, as I waited for the phone call that would let me know if I got the gig, I considered taking "Too Robust" as a name. It would have been my third traditional name. The first is one I inherited. The second, *Tahanku Sigsice*, is one I borrowed from my uncle. It means "he who has ugly brothers-in-law." But

112

"Too Robust" just didn't have any zing, or much of a story behind it. In any case, I did get the gig and an opportunity for another name—Two Left Moccasins. That was not the name of the character I was to portray; I had to wear two left Apache-style moccasins to play the part of a Cheyenne chief with no name. At any rate, those few days on the set of *Return to Lonesome Dove* proved to be pleasant and interesting, and this was how I joined the Cinema Tribe.

The call offering me the role came from Jon Voight in mid-August of 1993 while I was on my way home to Casper, Wyoming. (My wife promised that she didn't fall apart until after she hung up the phone). I had been recommended for the part by a mutual friend, John Wilder, who had written the screenplay for *Return to Lonesome Dove*. Among his other considerable credits is the screenplay for the miniseries *Centennial*. Previously, I had had the opportunity to work with and for John as a technical adviser on a project called *Lakota Moon*, a television movie about the Lakota filmed in Wyoming. (Unfortunately, that movie has not been aired in this country as of late 1995.) Because of this association I knew that John endeavors to portray Indians as people.

Some months before my audition for *Return to Lonesome Dove,* John Wilder had told me about the point in the story where the protagonist—Captain Woodrow Call—stumbles into a Cheyenne village, after having barely escaped from some angry Kiowa renegades. He is spent, nearly naked, and weaponless and has the audacity to ask the Cheyenne for their help. Help is given, but so is a lesson about honor from the Cheyenne chief.

Two Left Moccasins

Jon Voight was to play the part of Captain Call, taking over the part played by Tommy Lee Jones in *Lonesome Dove*. During a late-night call to his hotel room in Billings, Montana, we talked about the script and how the lesson imparted by the Cheyenne warrior added to the development of his character. Before the conversation I was only hopefully interested. Afterward *I wanted the part*. I was intrigued by Jon Voight's sense that his character's brief sojourn with Indians was as important as any other series of scenes, because Captain Call learns another definition of honor— especially as it relates to his illegitimate son.

My chances of not getting the part were greater than my chances of getting it. In addition to being "too robust," I had had no dramatic acting experience. But for whatever reason—probably because of Jon's insistence—I got the good news one Tuesday evening from Jon himself, and the next morning I was burning up I-25 and then I-90 to Billings.

The project was close to its sixtieth day and nearing the end of shooting when the Cheyenne camp segment was up. As many people know, movies are not shot in story sequence. So although our segment was one of the last to be shot, it comes somewhere near the middle of the film.

On Wednesday afternoon I reported to wardrobe, was measured for my leggings, and discovered that none of the buckskin shirts on the rack would fit. Either I was unusually large or wardrobe was under the impression that all Indians were small. This brief adventure in wardrobe reminded me of a previous brush with Hollywood, back on the Rosebud Sioux

Reservation. A casting person breezed through the res recruiting for extras to work in *Centennial.* He took one look at me and turned me down flat, shaking his head and muttering that I was far too tall to be an Indian. Until then, I had not been aware that race and ethnicity were defined by size. Then I wondered what the *minimum* height requirement was to be Indian, since I had apparently exceeded the *maximum.* Or what the sideways requirements were, for that matter (thinking that my brothers-in-law were borderline in that respect). Later, I was disappointed that I had not explained to him that I was good with my hands and had my stoic expressions down cold.

In any case, my measurements were taken for the shirt, and I headed next to a large table whose top was strewn with dozens of moccasins. To my dismay, my feet were nearly too big to be Indian, too—at least of the Plains variety. I dug through the pile but could find nothing that fit. Just as the wardrobe man was on the verge of making really snide remarks about my feet, a pair of Apache-style moccasins caught my eye. I wondered what Southwest moccasins were doing in among the wardrobe which was supposed to depict a Plains group. Waiting for me, as it turns out.

I grabbed one, saw that it was for the left foot, and tried it on. A perfect fit. I grabbed the other, saw that it was also for the left foot and did the only dignified thing I could think of. I removed the first moccasin from my left foot and tried the second one on the left foot, all the while scanning the table top in silent, prayerful desperation for a right, Apache-style, calf-length moccasin. There was none. And I also discovered that the second left moccasin was about one size larger than the first. What the hell, I thought, the audience will never know, and my feet will probably not be in any of the close-ups, Besides, I rationalized, if these were good enough for the Apaches, they're good enough for me. I put on my best I-planned-it-all-along face and handed the two left, Apache-style, not-the-same-size moccasins to the wardrobe man, trying not to think of the tracks I would leave in soft dirt.

The next morning got off to a more auspicious start, with a nearly twenty-mile ride to the set northwest of Billings with Jane Lind and Doris Leader Charge. Jane, an Eskimo from Alaska, (living in New York) has been an actress for twenty years. She was to play the role of Many Tears, my character's sister. Doris, a fellow Rosebud Sioux, was the Native American consultant for the project. She had been a language consultant for *Dances with Wolves* and had played the role of Pretty Shield in it.

Forty or so Northern Cheyenne and a few Crow who were hired to play the background were already on location when we arrived. I met them during and after the catered breakfast. Some of them had much more experience with this sort of thing than I did. I recognized some of the extras who had worked on *Lakota Moon* and was not surprised to learn that some of them had been in *Son of the Morning Star.*

In my dressing room I found my costume—a Plains-style buckskin shirt, a pair of leggings (which behaved more like hip waders), a breechclout, and, of course, two left Apache-style moccasins. I also found a sense of kinship with a group of people who can lay claim to a rare and unusual experience in the annals

Joseph Marshall III

of American filmmaking—Indians who have played Indians on screen. Jay Silverheels, Will Sampson, and Chief Dan George came immediately to mind. And of more recent vintage, August Shellenberg, Gordon Tootoosis, Graham Greene, Tantoo Cardinal, Rodney Grant, Jane Lind, Wes Studi, Doris Leader Charge, Floyd Westerman, and others. Not that I can compare myself in stature and ability to any of them, but thanks to all of them, I was about to add something new to my life (and my resume). And as I sat looking at my two left moccasins, with images and movie titles flashing through my mind, I began to reflect on various ethnic roles that had been played by actors in the past.

Ben Kingsley convinced me he was Gandhi, in *Gandhi*, Hugh Griffeth that he was a bedouin sheik in *Ben Hur*. But Trevor Howard couldn't convince me he was an old Cheyenne warrior in *Windwalker* any more than Burt Lancaster could persuade me he was Jim Thorpe in *Jim Thorpe: All-American*. Anthony Quinn was believable as Zorba in *Zorba the Greek* but not as Crazy Horse in *They Died with Their Boots On*. Victor Mature seemed more like a Roman centurion in *The Robe* than he appeared to be Crazy Horse in *Crazy Horse*.

Of course, I don't have the viewpoint of people from other cultures, but I can't help wonder what people in India thought of Kingley's portrayal of Gandhi, or how real bedouins reacted to Hugh Griffeth, and Greeks to Anthony Quinn, and Romans to Victor Mature. I suddenly began to understand why a non-Indian acquaintance of mine thought Anthony Quinn did just fine as an Indian (Native American) in *Nobody Loves a Drunken Indian* or that Robert Forster was just as believable in *Journey Through Rosebud*. Then it dawned on me that if in *Return to Lonesome Dove* I couldn't convince the viewer that I was at least an Indian on one level and a Cheyenne warrior on another, I'd be in deep trouble, though perhaps in good company. It's amazing what can cross one's mind when one is avoiding putting on two left moccasins.

Despite the two left moccasins, I knew I could basically look the part in that I was at least the same race as the character I was to portray. But why did Ben Kingsley come across as Gandhi in *Gandhi* and why did I feel insulted at Victor Mature's portrayal of Crazy Horse? Was it because of an outstanding job of makeup as opposed to a poor one? Was it the skill of the actors? I certainly think Kingsley portrayed Gandhi much better than Mature portrayed Crazy Horse. Perhaps the ultimate result in either case began with the casting of each actor. It was apparently easier for Kingsley to physically assume the character of Gandhi than it was for Mature to do the same with Crazy Horse. The obvious conclusion is that Mature was miscast. But why?

Both Gandhi and Crazy Horse are well-known historical figures, and one can assume that a wealth of information is available about both. Ultimately, did the lack of any photograph of Crazy Horse become a factor? Perhaps. Or was it the degree of sensitivity, both racial and political, that existed or did not exist at the time these actors were cast for their roles? To put it another way, who would it be least offensive to insult: a nation of nearly 900 million people and a prominent member of the world community or a nation of fifty thousand (at the time), within an ethnic minority with little political

Joseph Marshall III

clout that was less than 1 percent of the American population? Although none of these factors may have affected casting decisions in either case, in casting the role of Crazy Horse at that particular time, the producers could not have been unaware that any backlash resulting from miscasting or a bad portrayal of Crazy Horse would have been minimal at best.

The skill of an actor, as in the case of Ben Kingsley as Gandhi, and an appropriate makeup job certainly can contribute to a believable portrayal. In addition, if a convincing performance that includes accurate cultural representation is desired, then it is imperative that screenwriters, producers, and actors should not blatantly ignore facets of the culture being portrayed. Many Lakota snickered at Mature's portrayal of Crazy Horse as a verbose, melodramatic chief seemingly perpetually bedecked in a feather "war" bonnet. In reality, Crazy Horse was a quiet, painfully shy man who disdained even the simplest of ornamentation.

I was thankful that I was not being asked to portray a real person, but a little chagrined that my character had no name—and two left moccasins. Secretly I rationalized that since I at least looked the part, I was halfway there, even if I did leave weird footprints.

I decided it was time to join the Cinema Tribe. Dressed, I reported next to makeup and hair. I needed neither; however, in the makeup and hair trailer I watched Jon Voight as he sat in long johns and was turned into an emaciated and battered Captain Woodrow Call—complete with dried blood and bruises—under the skillful hand of the makeup artist. Between seemingly effortless deliveries of lines from the scenes we were to do later, he talked about how to make those scenes believable, worrying most about some of the dialogue to be spoken in Cheyenne. So was I. But, fortunately, one of the extras turned out to be a bilingual teacher who spoke fluent Cheyenne.

Having worked on *Lakota Moon,* I was somewhat familiar with all of the preparation and the number of people working behind the scenes. But here I was not part of the crew; I was part of the cast. In a sense, I was part of something that really didn't exist, and it would be my job to help turn John Wilder's script into flesh and blood, heart and soul, so the story could exist in the perception of the viewer. When that happened, it would be no longer John Wilder's script. It would be Woodrow Call with sore feet, a battered body, and a frontier white man's audacity to ask for help from Indians who had little to give. It would be a Cheyenne woman's quiet perseverance in spite of pain and haunting memories. A Cheyenne warrior's anger and dignity, and his contempt for the symbol of all that had changed his world. And somehow there would be an understanding. A brief connection that would transcend righteous Cheyenne anger and strip away white audacity to teach that honor and courage were not the exclusive virtue of one race or another. A connection on the common ground of humanity. If only such common ground could be found in the real world.

I looked into the piercing blue eyes of the man across the tiny room and saw the soul of Captain Woodrow Call. I looked inside myself, searched, and felt The Warrior emerging (perhaps reemerging). He was wearing two left moccasins and had no name, but he was there. The blue eyes were no longer intimidating. John Wilder's script was coming to life. In my mind's eye I could see an injured and exhausted Captain Woodrow Call being guided toward The Warrior by two younger warriors, herded through the crowd of curious Cheyenne men, women, and children. I (The Warrior) stand firm to meet him.

> *Call approaches the Warrior.*
>
> CALL
> *I need a horse.*
>
> WARRIOR
> *What happen—you?*
>
> CALL
> *I run arrows—Kiowa.*
> *(Warrior explains to the other men in Cheyenne.)*
>
> CALL
> *I need a horse!*
> *Call collapses at The Warrior's feet.*

The Cheyenne village was nestled on a bench above a dry creek bed, between two ridges thick with pine. It was at least a quarter mile up from base camp. As I walked the already well-worn trail to the village, I resisted looking back at the tracks I was leaving and imagined myself going back into a different time. A dolly track, already set up down the middle of the row of lodges, kept 1993 connected like a wasp on a string, droning angrily on the periphery. In a moment I was able to imagine it away, sending it and the already scurrying crew to the outer reaches of my awareness:

Two Left Moccasins

The only thing in my focus were the costumed extras, who became some Cheyenne of 1870-something instead of 1993. The children looked at me curiously as I walked to the end of the row of lodges. Some of the women looked up and smiled shyly. Here and there a man nodded a polite and dignified greeting. Some things don't change, I thought. Except for the passage of time and some unimaginably difficult circumstances along the way, these people were the same. Then in the corner of my eye I saw a young mother pull a disposable diaper out of a leather case. But I instantaneously sent that to the outer reaches, too. It wasn't until I saw Captain Woodrow Call walking along the dolly track in a bathrobe that 1993 weakened my connection to 1870-something. But the connection wasn't entirely broken. It still isn't.

In December of 1992, I had participated in an international conference on historic travel corridors in Natchitoches, (pronounced *knack-a-dish)* Louisiana. The moderator for my group had asked each of us to describe ourselves in one sentence. My description was a *primitive trapped in the twentieth century.* I felt that way as I stood at the end of the dolly track and let the sights and sounds of the moment return—the large camera sliding down the track on a practice run and assistant directors shouting instructions. The Cinema Tribe certainly lived in a different world. I realized now that my first glimpse of it had been when I was a child. Although I hadn't fully realized it at the time.

As a child I had watched several episodes of *The Lone Ranger* with *"his faithful Indian companion, Tonto."* My diligent attention to several episodes as an adult failed to reveal any clue as to Tonto's particular tribe or group, and the stories had seemed so much more real the few times I watched as a child. I do recall paying particularly close attention for a time to the Lakota adults in my life to see how many times they said "heap big" or "get-um." None of them knew what *Kemosabe* meant, so I was reasonably certain it was not a Lakota word that was secretly divulged to Tonto. No Lakota adult ever said "heap big" or "get-um" in the normal course of speaking English, or "Ugh," for that matter. The only adult who ever did was a male, non-Indian teacher who said that I had done a "heap good job" on an assignment. And the (hopefully) well-meaning acquaintance who told me recently that it was time to "get-um some coffee, chief." Of course, he was the same man who was "so surprised" that I spoke English so well. Anyway, I concluded that Tonto was really a white man, and that was the reason his tribe was not mentioned. In a sense, I was close. Jay Silverheels, the actor who played Tonto, was Indian. On the other hand, Tonto was a manifestation of Indian in the mind of at least one non-Indian television writer—a manifestation based more on imagination and racial bias than reality.

Jay Silverheels was one of the early inductees into the Cinema Tribe, and his *Tonto* character certainly was the personification of Indian for at least one generation of non-Indian television viewers and the perpetuation of a stereotype. He came to life in a period when, in the mind of white American society, the Indian had already been subjugated. Therefore, Tonto was the image of the current status of Indians in America, without regard for the real image of Indians in the time setting of the Lone Ranger stories—the latter part of the 1800s. During that era many tribes in the West were doing everything possible to avoid contact with whites or were locked in a death struggle over territory and their own very existence. Assimilation, or the process of turning Indians into whites, was in full swing in the 1950s and 1960s. As a reflection of this, Tonto walked one step behind the Lone Ranger, and his horse (Scout) was not as fast or noble as the Lone Ranger's horse (Silver); Tonto used a six-gun rather than bows and arrows and rode in a saddle. Even the name of Tonto's horse was descriptive of his relationship to his white companion. Tonto's one apparent connection to his Indian identity was a thin leather headband, never mind that most Indians of the day had never heard of one. Overall, the message was that Indians were acceptable as long as they endeavored to be like whites and kept their place and distance.

Tonto's apparent calling was to have saved a white man's life and to thereafter function as his *faithful Indian companion*. His association with the white hero gave him "credibility," since he worked to preserve white values of justice and fair play. However, the faithful companion syndrome obscured, for millions of television viewers then and now, a lesson in reality: that Indians can function in a non-Indian setting. Though Tonto was the personification of a white person's concept of Indian, Jay Silverheels functioned and, apparently, succeeded in an environment totally foreign to Indians of the day. This is in keeping with the fact that as a whole white society of the day was also foreign to Indians, who were still in the midst of societal changes brought on by the reservation era.

Joseph Marshall III

The Cinema Tribe may live in a bizarre environment, but, in a way, it is no stranger than many real environments Indians have to function in daily. Many real Indians, such as the following people, have not only functioned in an environment different than their own, they have succeeded: Ada Deer, the Menominee who is the current commissioner of Indian affairs and runs the Bureau of Indian Affairs; Maria Tallchief, the Cherokee ballet dancer; Wilma Mankiller, the visionary chairwoman of the Cherokee Tribe of Oklahoma; Carlos Rainwater, the Miccosoukee who served on the National Board of Governors of the American Red Cross; Scott Ratliff, an Eastern Shoshoni who is an educator and also served several terms in the Wyoming House of Representatives; Lloyd Moses, a Rosebud Sioux who rose to the rank of major general in the United States Army; and Dr. Lorenzo Stars, a young Rosebud Sioux physician working on his home reservation. Of course, there are many, many more Indians in prominent positions in all walks of life throughout this country spanning several generations, with many more yet to come.

To be a "Tonto" is distasteful to Indians because of the obvious connotation that the only worthwhile Indian is one who is subservient to whites. Tonto certainly was subservient to the Lone Ranger. However, I doubt if Jay Silverheels was subservient to the actor who played the title role. But if he was treated as an inferior, it was a difficult price to pay for being a member of the Cinema Tribe. I have yet to meet the Indian person who wants to be a "Tonto"; but there are many who speak fondly and respectfully of Jay Silverheels.

Two Left Moccasins

One of my favorite movie characters of all time is Lodgeskins in *Little Big Man,* played by Chief Dan George. It was probably the first conscious effort by a feature movie production to humanize an Indian. If it wasn't intended that way, then I'm pleased that no one impeded Dan George's portrayal.

Dan George, obviously, was the greater part of Lodgeskins—witty and wise, with a sense of humor—traits that also describe all of my grandparents, who were still alive when the movie was released. None of them was stone-faced or stoic and certainly not given to monosyllabic pronouncements. When I saw the twinkle in Lodgeskin's eyes, I saw my grandfathers. When I saw him take his blindness in stride, there were both of my grandmothers enduring debilitating illnesses with dignity and without complaint.

Dan George's Lodgeskins was better than Anthony Quinn's and Victor Mature's portrayals of Crazy Horse. Better than Dame Judith Anderson's Buffalo Cow Head in *Man Called Horse*, better than Burt Lancaster's Jim Thorpe, and better than several other examples that were as much a result of miscasting as they were based on ignorance of the reality of being Indian, both historically and contemporarily. Better because Dan George's own humanity overwhelmed any dramatic posturings or any stereotypical dark savagery expected of Lodgeskins. And Dan George's humanity is a reality in the personalities of old Indian men and women, then and now, much more than bloodcurdling cries, brandished tomahawks, and lips curled in savage sneers. But over the years, because there were more than just a few movies where non-Indians were cast as

Joseph Marshall III

Indians and played a role based on a non-Indian writer's lack of factual and realistic perception of Indians, that kind of Indian became indelibly imprinted on the psyche of the moviegoing public. All of this dawned on me several years ago as I watched *Little Big Man* on video. I wondered how many non-Indian movie afficionados who have seen it think that Lodgeskins was misportrayed by Dan George. I wondered how many non-Indians were genuinely surprised at Lodgeskins's sense of humor and/or dismissed it as a misrepresentation.

Jay Silverheels and Dan George were pioneers of the Cinema Tribe. The reasons for casting them in their particular roles were probably different. But, in the long run, whatever those reasons might have been pale in comparison to the fact that each of them proved that Indians were and are capable as screen actors whether we portray a non-Indian's Indian—such as Tonto—or an Indian's Indian—such as Kicking Bird in *Dances with Wolves.* Jay Silverheels might have had to endure some indignity, not to mention a jibe or two from the Indian community, because he played a caricature of an Indian. But at a most essential level he proved that Indians can portray Indians on screen (and on stage). And should. Dan George stepped through the door opened by Jay Silverheels and showed that Indians can portray Indians as Indians really were or are, so long as it is allowed and enabled. This brings us to a consideration of the parameters of current Indian film roles and the question of what constitutes an Indian movie.

Return to Lonesome Dove is a story that revolves around one man's sense of honor, and on the whole it is a story of Euro-Americans. There happen to be characters in the story who are Indian: a half-Cherokee, half-Black villian, some Kiowa renegades, and the no-name Cheyenne leader with his sister Many Tears. There is factual, historical basis for all these characters, and all are basically important to the plot. But these factors do not make it an "Indian movie." Neither—as far as I am concerned—were *Dances with Wolves* and *Last of the Mohicans*, in spite of the fact that both had significant Indian roles and both stories could not have been told without Indians on screen. They are not "Indian movies" for the reason that the plots of the stories were not Indian and they did not revolve around a central Indian character.

It is understandable that many people regard *Dances with Wolves* as the "best Indian movie ever made." As far as I am concerned, an Indian movie has yet to be made, although I do think *Dances with Wolves* has become the standard as far as the portrayal of Indians. Indian actors were cast to play Indians, the Indian actors turned in skillful and professional performances, Indian stunt performers and Indian technical advisors were used, and there was more than the usual lackadaisical attention to cultural and historical accuracy. If *Little Big Man* took a shaky step in the direction of more accurate portrayals of Indians and Indian history, *Dances with Wolves* took a very firm step.

Geronimo: An American Legend took something of a step in that direction simply because a title role in a feature film was played by an Indian actor, but it falls short because the screenplay did not depart from the more familiar territory of hiding behind a non-Indian

Joseph Marshall III

character to tell an Indian story—as did *Dances with Wolves.* Despite the fact that these films are better than so many others in their genre, neither *Geronimo: An American Legend* nor *Dances with Wolves* is an Indian movie.

Two other films in which Indian characters have more significant on-screen time and are more central to the plot are *Nobody Loves a Drunken Indian* and *Clear Cut.* However, despite these positive aspects, they are still not Indian movies because the primary creative force and control behind them is not Indian. In other words the stories or screenplays were not developed and/or written by Indian writers, and the filming was not directed by Indian filmmakers.

An area where Indian screenwriters and directors are at work is in the less publicized field of documentary filmmaking. One of the best examples of such an Indian film is *Surviving Columbus,* directed by Diane Reyna, from Taos Pueblo in New Mexico. Therefore, it cannot be said that Indians have not yet entered that segment of the film industry. It only remains for Indian screenwriters and directors to broaden and enrich their experience, hone their skills, and bring more Indians into those particular professions.

Indian writers have been a part of the American literary scene since about the turn of the century, taking advantage of that creative medium to express Indian points of view to readers. By contrast, moviegoers by and large have not had the opportunity to see and hear untainted, honest, Indian viewpoints in films—though there have been occasional glimpses.

Kicking Bird in *Dances With Wolves* telling Dunbar that the trail of a "true human being" is the best one to follow, for example. Lodgeskins telling Jack Crabb something similar when he says, "There is only a limited number of human beings." Or when Uncas and Chingachkook offer thanks to the elk they have killed in the opening scenes of *The Last of the Mohicans*. And when Geronimo tells an angry Mangas that the real enemy are the whites and not the Apache scouts who were duped into their service in one of the final scenes of *Geronimo: An American Legend*.

When Indian screenwriters and directors achieve more recognition and increased opportunities to offer their creative efforts in the same way Indian novelists and scholars have done, true Indian viewpoints will have found yet another form of expression. And *Indian movies* will be made.

There was a time when I thought Indian screen actors who played Indian parts that were the result of non-Indian perceptions of what Indians really were had somehow forsaken their "Indianness" or insulted their own kind. Then I began to think that perhaps they had gotten into acting for the same reasons anyone else does—to make a living and achieve recognition. Both very human motives. Reluctantly, I then conceded that perhaps they were trying to make the statement that Indians can be a part of every facet of the American mainstream—that they can give a day's work for a day's pay, like many Indians do daily in numerous other professions (with the exception of my brothers-in-law, of course). Whatever the motivation, it could not have

been easy at first for such actors when opportunities
were severely limited by the lack of Indian roles and
producers and directors were casting speaking parts
with Italians, Hispanics, or Asians. When I consider
those realities, the expression "Cinema Tribe" ceases to
be a facetious epithet, especially after opportunities to
meet a few Indian actors. None of these actors have
forsaken their "Indianness" and some of them are trying
to become more aware of their tribal heritage. Instead,
for me the Cinema Tribe has become a very special
club. And on a warm day one August I endeavored to be
a member in good standing.

It is the trading scene. The Warrior has sent
for Captain Woodrow Call and waits for him on a
buffalo robe beneath a rock overhang. The Warrior
plans to barter his sister Many Tears's future for a rifle
and a horse.

As the stand-ins leave and I take my spot on the
buffalo robe, my worst fear is realized. My feet will be in
the wide shot. There, for most of the world to see will be
a Cheyenne warrior, a leader of his small band, wearing
two left Apache-style moccasins.

For a panic-stricken second I am more
concerned with two left moccasins than with my lines, or
being The Warrior. But suddenly, The Warrior emerges,
telling me that he had traded with the Apache sometime
long ago. They were poor, too, and needed food. So a
man traded all that he had—two left moccasins—so that
his family could eat for a few more days. The
actor responds, reasoning that if he kept one foot back,
no one would see it.

Two Left Moccasins

Panic leaves. I look over at my new friend, Jon Voight, as I see Captain Woodrow Call emerging. The Warrior is ready to trade.

Beneath a rock overhang, seated on a buffalo robe.

CALL
I don't need no woman.

WARRIOR
You need horse, you want. You take woman, too.

CALL
I can't care for her!

WARRIOR
You came without fear. She trust you.

CALL
I can't!

WARRIOR
Must be...

That evening as I walked back down toward the base camp, I turned for just a moment to glance at my tracks. There clearly, were two left footprints. The tracks of a warrior.

To all the world, my (very) minor role in *Return to Lonesome Dove* may have no name. In the cast of characters he is listed as The Warrior. But to me he is Two Left Moccasins. A man with a heart and a mind. One who has left a clear and strong trail. Someday, perhaps, I will do the same.

I may never play another movie role. Even if I do, the three days on the set of *Return to Lonesome Dove*

Joseph Marshall III

will always be a special memory. Jane Lind and Jon Voight taught me a lesson or two about their craft as well as about themselves. And I know that the opportunity may never have come about had it not been for my friends John Wilder and Jon Voight, and their quiet efforts to cast Indian actors to portray Indians in the movies. But I also owe a debt of gratitude to people like Jane Lind, Graham Greene, Floyd Westerman, Doris Leader Charge, Tantoo Cardinal, Chief Dan George, Jay Silverheels, and a host of others with distinguished and easily recognizable names. With their dedication and professionalism, they have proven, beyond a shadow of a doubt, that there is an overwhelming logic in casting Indians to portray Indians.

One of the strongest memories from my sojourn in filmmaking is of the final moments in my dressing room, before I shed my costume. Images, movie titles, and scenes from them flashed through my mind on a never-ending loop. For a brief time I had been a member of the Cinema Tribe and had enjoyed it. For some reason, it was very difficult to reach down and unlace those two left moccasins.

Voices in the Wind

I can hear one of my favorite storytellers, my maternal grandfather, as he creates a world where Iktomi, the Trickster, learns yet another life lesson.

It is a windy day as Iktomi wanders across the prairie toward the river looking for his next meal. From the trees along the water he hears what seems to be an argument. Always curious, Iktomi seeks the source of the apparent disagreement and finds it. Two tall cottonwood saplings, being swayed by the strong wind, are rubbing against one another, moaning and groaning as they do. Of course, Iktomi, ever the mediator, beseeches the two trees to stop their fighting. They ignore him, but he persists. He rants and raves against the evils of fighting and the virtues of neighborliness. The two cottonwoods increase their wailing as the wind blows harder. Not to be ignored and convinced that he is right, Iktomi decides to take a drastic step. He puts his hand in between the trees to prevent them from rubbing against one another and eliminate the reason for their arguments. At that precise moment, the wind stops blowing, and Iktomi is caught between the trees. Though he pulls and struggles with all of his might, he cannot free himself. He yells at the trees to release him, he begs, he ridicules, he threatens to make firewood of them, but all to no avail. They ignore him, and he is stuck. For days Iktomi stands with his hand caught between the trees. He is terribly hungry and cannot lay down to rest. Though he occasionally pleads and threatens, nothing happens until the wind starts blowing again. And as the wind comes and moves the trees, Iktomi is able to remove his hand. As he staggers away he tells the trees they can argue for the rest of their lives for all he cares.

In telling this story, my maternal grandfather was, of course, trying to teach me that it is better to mind one's own business.

There are moments in my life when a voice from the past resonates so clearly in my memory that I expect someone to be standing nearby. Many times it is the voice of a grandparent. One of them has come and gone, again, like the last, too fleeting blink of a sunset. Sometimes I reach out a hand in a woefully inadequate gesture of acknowledgment because I still miss them so. After a moment, though sadness mingles with the silence, there is no emptiness. They filled my world with their presence when they were here and are still a part of it because of the memories I have of each of them, especially when one of their voices comes in the wind. This kind of connection is, I think, especially meaningful to Indians or Native Americans because of one of the strongest aspects of our various cultures—the oral tradition.

Native American oral tradition is a mechanism for both perpetuating culture and preserving the past. It enables a given group or society to endure from one generation to the next by passing on all the elements that preserve structure and purpose while providing a sense of history. Yet the process is so woven into everyday life that there are moments when an individual may not be aware that it is being utilized. For example, the story of a communal buffalo hunt may contain specific information on how a horse-mounted hunter approached his quarry, how the dead animals were butchered and the meat was prepared for cooking and drying. The same story is repeated verbatim several times. Therefore, not only is the listener becoming familiar with (often empirical) anecdotal information about an actual event, he or she is also beginning to learn how buffalo are hunted on horseback and how to process and prepare the meat. Thus, a bit of family history and critically important skills are taught simultaneously through the medium of a good and well-told story. But the value of this tradition has still further implications. The listener will pass the story on to his or her children and grandchildren, adding his or her own specific experiences in support of its basic theme *without* changing the story. Despite generation after generation of retelling as long as memory serves, the original story will always be attributed to the original storyteller, and there will always be continuity of content.

Oral tradition relies on many stories, and its strength comes from the fact that families are made up of individuals, communities (villages or encampments) are made up of families, and bands or tribes are made up of communities. Therefore, one story is not, by any means, insignificant.

One of the most immediate questions about oral traditions from even the most well-meaning non-Indians, concerns its reliability. Invariably, the example of the children's game of passing whispered information along a circle of players, from one to the next, is the basic reference. More often than not, in such a game, the information is changed by the time it reaches the last player. For many non-Indians, it serves as the most logical and compelling argument against the reliability—and therefore the credibility— of oral tradition. Such an argument may raise questions regarding oral tradition, but it is also an implicit affirmation of the apparent total reliability of the written word. (This type of thinking is unfortunately the basis for condescending opinions regarding other aspects of Native American cultures.) To casually dismiss the basic mechanism by which a culture has endured for many centuries by likening it to a children's game is ludicrous, ethnocentric, and narrow-minded; it is indicative of a total lack of awareness regarding oral tradition.

The best way for me to answer criticism about the reliability and credibility of oral tradition is to use my maternal grandparents as examples. Both had many stories to tell because stories were the foundation for the lessons they wanted to impart. And the hallmark of the stories was consistency.

There were stories about trust, being cautious, not interfering in others' affairs, the fallacy and danger of making judgments based only on the obvious (in white society not "judging a book by its cover"), respect, honesty, and perseverence. Many of these lessons were contained in the numerous Iktomi or Trickster stories, but the experiences or adventures of an ancestor were also used in similar fashion. There were the general family biographies with many specific anecdotes about relatives and ancestors. And, of course, there were the stories regarding important past events, such as a memorable tribal gathering, a natural disaster, or a battle. The common denominator for all of these stories was consistency—regardless of the purpose or length, the stories were told the same way each time, without alteration or embellishment. The only exception was when the storyteller's memory began to fade, and in such instances, he or she would simply say "I can't remember." There was no speculation as to what the story might have been but simply an admission of loss of memory. At such moments, the young listener was so familiar with the story from having heard it on previous occasions that he or she could fill in the blanks. Many times in my grandfather's later years, when he paused during a story and looked toward me, I would simply say, "Remember, Grandpa, you said it was...." He would smile and nod and go on with the story. The mechanism was working. The stories were not only being passed on, they were being passed on intact in their original form. That original form may well have dated back several generations.

There are also other aspects of consistency in the oral tradition. A story's character and tone were kept intact because of a particular form of delivery—voice inflections, pauses, and hand gestures. And sometimes the setting where a story was repeatedly told was the same—a particular type of environment or a specific place. Because of such consistencies, stories lived on, remaining relevant and vibrant on

Joseph Marshall III

several levels. They embodied voices from the past, resonating with depth, with their own life, and losing little, if anything, from one generation to the next.

To pre-reservation Indian cultures, oral tradition was an obvious and logical way to pass on information, knowledge, and skills. It was a system that worked well without the medium through which you are reading this essay. But that is not to say that some form of communication using signs and symbols did not exist. The Incas, Mayans, and Toltecs developed highly sophisticated cuneiform and hieroglyphic forms of writing that are only now being deciphered. Further to the north, other cultures developed simpler but no less effective methods of communicating with symbols. A few examples are the cermonial belts (often called wampum) of the Iroquois and Algonquin peoples, which were made from quahog clamshells fashioned into white and purple beads and strung in a manner to record significant family and tribal events; or the calendar posts of the Tohono O'odham, saguaro cactus ribs with a series of cuts and slashes that chronicled important events. These methods of recording were very similar in purpose to the winter counts of several Plains tribes, which consisted of a series of sketches on a tanned bison, elk, or deer hide recording the most significant event of a given year. Such mechanisms required comprehension and interpretation of the symbols and pictures used—just as reading does. If reading is an interpretation of symbols into speech sounds, then it would be difficult to argue that interpreting the symbols and images on a wampum belt, a calendar post, or a winter count was not reading. But since human societies and institutions constantly evolve, wampum belts, calendar posts, and winter counts were indeed precursors to more developed systems that inevitably would have appeared. And they certainly were a progression from simple symbols drawn in the earth or on cave walls. Still, the existence and use of such mechanisms did not render oral tradition obsolete; oral tradition was not affected until the time of European influence and interference. Even today, many of us forget that oral communication is still significant and necessary—fax machines and E-mail notwithstanding. Wampum belts, calendar posts, and winter counts were interpreted and explained. Without such interpretation they were merely signs, symbols, and pictures. On the other hand, a good storyteller can create vivid images without drawing or writing signs, symbols, and pictures. If we did not have reading and writing in this society, the value, validity, and reliabiltiy of oral communication would be immediately evident.

A scene from the movie *Black Robe* depicts an instance where the Iroquois of 1646 are awed by a Frenchman who reads something written by another Frenchman and reveals information previously known only to one of the Indians until he tells the writer. The scene gives the impression that writing is a far superior form of communication and that Indians are awed by it because they have nothing that can compare to it. They could not understand the symbols used by the Frenchman. This is an example of the usual European ethnocentric assumption that any aspect of a "civilized" culture is easily better than anything a tribal culture can produce. I beg to differ.

Joseph Marshall III

I recall a time when my grandfather and I had just climbed a difficult, steep slope. At the top of the hill, just a mile or so north of the Little White River, we paused to rest. He looked around on either side of the old trail we had followed and finally located three fist-sized stones, which he speculated had been dislodged by cattle and now were hidden in the grass by many seasons of growth. My grandfather gathered the stones and placed them in a line perpendicular to the trail, explaining that these stones always had been here as markers. Placed in the manner he had replaced them, they were a sign that the trail going down from the top of the hill was difficult. A traveler following this particular trail from the north would be warned if he understood the sign. When I asked why he had replaced the stones, he indicated that someone might still know their meaning.

The question that did not dawn on my seven-year-old perception was how long those stones might have been there. About twenty years ago, a cousin and I rode to the top of that same hill. The stones were gone, but so were those who could have read and understood their message. However, chances are that some riders had seen them there before they disappeared and had wondered about their significance and who had placed them there. That probably would have been the extent of any curiosity, and no rider would have known that someone was trying to deliver a message from across the span of decades, perhaps centuries—simply because he would not have known the meaning of a symbol. Are we to assume then that a person who failed to understand one symbol is generally inferior or ignorant?

Voices in the Wind

Such assumptions were readily made by those who endeavored to actively separate the Indian from his culture, using them as the justification for the policy and process of assimilation. Henry Pratt, a former army officer and the superintendent of the Carlisle Indian School in Carlisle, Pennsylvania, around the turn of the century, saw his duty to be "to kill the Indian and save the man." Such attitudes and intentions were the hallmark of the United States government's policy of assimilation, the goal of which was to transform Indians into acceptable versions of Euro-Americans. This was a philosophy and policy that was totally supported by missionary groups working on Indian reservations who had built and operated boarding schools.

The process of assimilation was successful in destroying many aspects of Indian cultures, and any aspect not destroyed completely suffered some kind of damage. Languages probably were affected most severely. Today, of the approximately four hundred ethnically identifiable tribes still surviving, about 145 still use their native languages to the extent that they can be regarded as living languages. Of course, that means over half of all tribes in the United States have lost their languages. Furthermore, some tribes are still struggling to save languages that continue to be endangered—such as the Northern Arapaho on the Wind River Reservation in Wyoming and the Mandan of the Three Affiliated Tribes on the Fort Berthold Reservation in North Dakota. Such language loss is due entirely to the fact that government- and church-operated schools actively suppressed the use of native languages by Indian students—because language is one of the most obvious aspects of culture.

Joseph Marshall III

To deny a group of people their own language is to deny them their own culture. As early as the late 1800s both government- and church-operated boarding shools for Indians (both on and off the reservation, with one of the latter being Carlisle Indian School in Carlisle, Pennsylvania) often kept their students away from home for the entire school year. This practice separated young Indians from primary native languages in the home spoken by parents and grandparents; and it coincided with harshly enforced rules against the use of native language on school grounds during the school year. In too many instances, the extent of the loss of several aspects of a culture can be directly correlated to the extent of the loss of language. And the policy and practice of denying use of their languages to Indian students from many different tribes had an enormous impact on many aspects of Indian cultures. One aspect that suffered extensive damage is oral tradition. Today, although the mechanism of oral tradition is still largely intact, the essence is not the same. Listening to the story of a communal buffalo hunt told in English is never the same as listening to it told in Lakota.

Indian tribes know, however, that the efforts to kill the Indian and save the man have not totally succeeded. Thankfully, numerous aspects of many cultures have survived to this day. But any sense of victory must be tempered with the knowledge that many languages and many cultures have been irretrievably lost. And we must resolve to never let it happen again. One way to assure this is to reinstate oral tradition to its rightful place among our cultures. Those groups and tribes which are fortunate to still have a living language must be the leaders in this effort. Those tribes which lost their languages can still remember the stories. The loss of a certain essence to a story is better than losing the story entirely.

In recent years, Indian narratives relating to certain historical events have come under renewed scrutiny by some people who had previously regarded them as unimportant and unreliable because of their apparent esoteric nature and because they derived from oral tradition. Oral history was dismissed by most people as folk tales simply because it could not reach as wide an audience as the written word of Euro-Americans. Now, however, there is debate among certain non-Indian historians about the accuracy of certan Indian narratives, and some groups and individuals are reexamining such narratives—a trend that began with a grass fire at one historical site.

In 1983, a prairie fire swept over a significant portion of the Little Bighorn Battlefield National Monument—then still known as Custer Battlefield National Monument. This presented an opportunity for archaeologists to examine and analyze exposed artifacts, notably shell casings. But most importantly, the patterns of distribution and locations of shell casings provided solid clues as to the probable positions of combatants. To the surprise of many—except Indians knowledgeable about the Battle of the Little Bighorn—the distribution and locations of shell casings corroborated Indian versions of the battle. Thirteen years later, the debate among non-Indian historians and archaeologists still sputters now and again. Some are still reluctant to give credence to Indian narratives of the

Joseph Marshall III

144

battle. Suffice it to say that among Indians there was no debate as to the veracity of Indian accounts, because there was no doubt regarding the significance of oral tradition.

Since 1876 many Indian participants of the battle have been interviewed by non-Indians. A few of the Indian scouts who rode with the Seventh Cavalry have given depositions. In short, there is a body of empirical, anecdotal information which has been available for many years. However, there is much more that is available since not all of the Indian participants have given interviews to non-Indians.

In 1896, twenty years after the battle, a thirty-eight-year-old Lakota decided to disclose the details of his participation in it to his family, mainly because he was dying of Spanish influenza. To his wife and eight-year-old son, he described how he had been involved in the repulsion of the first attack (Reno's assault on the Hunkpapa encampment). Furthermore, he provided details regarding actions and events in which he was involved or that unfolded near his location. But he concluded his stories with the strict warning not to disclose the information to any white person and certainly not to anyone connected with the government. It was the very real fear of reprisal from the government which had prevented him from disclosing the details of his participation in the "Greasy Grass Fight," as he called it. Twenty years later that fear had not diminished, and it was the reason for the strict warning to his wife and son.

Considering that there were possibly as many as ten thousand Lakota and Cheyenne people present when the battle took place, and most of them were old enough to make detailed observations of some event or

Voices in the Wind

another, the narratives put on the written record are only a small part of the many stories that still exist. Yet it appears that many historians are ignoring those stories, focusing primarily on narratives already recorded. Perhaps this is just as well, for two reasons. First, many of the unrecorded narratives have been passed down via the mechanism of oral tradition, sometimes with the admonition to be cautious about revealing them to the wrong people, and sometimes only with an extracted promise that the story never be revealed except to preserve it from one generation to the next. Second, myths die hard. In spite of new archaeological evidence which is debunking many non-Indian versions of the battle, there are some who stubbornly cling to those versions. It is entirely possible that Indian narratives which support other versions in whole or in part might be used selectively as corroborative material. To be fair, Indian narratives of events that included participation of non-Indians should be regarded as significant and independent versions of that event, not as subordinate to non-Indian versions. Both versions should be accorded equal status until and unless one is proven to be in error. And at least in one instance, a fire at the Little Bighorn Battlefield National Monument seems to have done just that.

Whatever any debate may be among non-Indian historians, archaeologists, and ethnologists regarding Indian oral tradition, it must be understood that the foremost purpose of Indian oral tradition is to function as an integral part of Indian cultures. And it can be a mechanism, in this day and age, to enable Indians to reconnect with their individual tribal identities and

Joseph Marshall III

to strengthen the overall identity shared by the various indigenous groups on this continent. Some call it the pan-Indian identity.

One way in which non-Indians have helped establish and reinforce pan-Indian identity, whether intentionally or not, is by putting stories, statements, and speeches of notable Indian people on the record. This has occurred through first-person interviews, at public ceremonies where Indians were invited to speak, and at treaty negotiations and signings. Such records of stories, statements, and speeches can be regarded as part of the pan-Indian oral tradition, even if they have reached us in a rather convoluted way. Of more importance than the manner of conveyance is the fact that Indian wisdom, feelings, and insight from people of different tribes and different times are available to us in the here and now. An excellent, composite source of some of these records is the book *Touch the Earth: A Self-portrait of Indian Existence* compiled by T.C. McCluhan and published by Simon and Schuster. The recording of Indian thought in writing, whatever the forum for expression, has been happening since Europeans came. While some non-Indians think that it has had a significant impact on the preservation of Indian cultures, I do not agree with that assessment. Indian cultures survived to the extent that they did because Indian people did what was necessary to preserve them—sometimes under threat of and in spite of punishment. For example, my father was severely punished for daring to speak Lakota on the grounds of a government boarding school in the 1930s. There were certainly many other incidents of this nature.

If direct punishment was not meted out, apathy certainly was. In my early elementary school years, I recall an occasion when I finally summoned up the nerve to tell my grandfather's version of the Battle of the Little Bighorn in class. Before I was finished, the teacher's response was that it "was nice, but we shall stick to the real story." Though her response and the attitude toward Indian oral history it represented was certainly discouraging, it did not diminish my faith in Lakota oral tradition.

In the past few years I have answered questions from many people regarding the mechanism of oral tradition. Some focused on the reliability and credibility of oral history; others pertained to the viability of oral tradition, suggesting in a backhanded way that oral tradition must be saved by the conveyance of stories, biographies, histories, ceremonies, spiritual beliefs, societal roles, and crafting methods and practices to a written, audio, and visual record. By contrast, some Indian people are fearful that doing so would destroy oral a tradition itself. Such debate seems to highlight fundamental questions concerning oral tradition: which is more important, the tradition or the content? Or is Indian oral tradition in any real danger of being lost? For an answer, we should consider how one of the most obvious aspects of Indian cultures remains viable to this day—dancing.

Every summer and increasingly over the winter months, there are major Indian powwows or celebrations in this country either on reservations or in metropolitan areas. The Indian powwow has for some become an expression of a pan-Indian identity. Therefore, not only

Joseph Marshall III

has dancing survived, it is also thriving and evolving. Nevertheless, some traditionalists in the Indian community fear that specific tribal dances are being forgotten or altered by the current trend toward dancing competitions for prize money. The phenomenon of dancing contests certainly has been responsible for the newest form of dance, which is the "fancy dance" for both men and women.

It is difficult to pinpoint which Indian community or tribe first conducted a dance contest for money and/or prizes. But once it occurred, it caught on quickly. At most large powwows, dancing is generally categorized into social dancing (wherein anyone, including uncostumed spectators, are invited to dance), demonstrations of specific tribal dances, honoring dances (associated with giveaways, naming ceremonies, and so forth), and the dancing contests. The dance competitions are divided into categories based on age, gender, and style—for example, age twelve and under girls' traditional, or women's shawl, or men's traditional. The number of categories is often dictated by the amount of prize money available, but the two basic categories are "traditional" and "fancy."

Traditional dancing is any dance associated with specific, culturally authentic forms of dance, such as shawl dances for women and sneak-up dances for men. Traditional dancers must wear appropriate traditional costumes, such as tanned and quilled or beaded dresses for women and eagle feather bustles for men (the twin fan of feathers worn on the small of the back that opens outward).

The evolvement of culture is dependent on the evolvement of specific aspects of that culture. Indian dancing has evolved to contests because individual competition is an important aspect of most Indian cultures. Recognition certainly is a desirable incentive and reward for participating in a contest. Payment of money also increases the sense of competition and the number of contestants. Moreover, these incentives have spurred the evolvement of a dance form—fancy dancing.

Fancy dancing, for both men and women, is an intensely athletic event which is made more compelling by splendidly colorful costumes. To be a man or woman fancy dancer, one must be extremely physically coordinated and have a sense of style. Fancy dancing is fast steps to fast drumming; it begins at a rapid pace and gradually intensifies. Suffice it to say, there are not many old fancy dancers.

Fancy dancing continues to gain in popularity as more and more powwows offer ever bigger cash prizes and promote fancy dancing as the featured contest. However, at each powwow there is still a large contingent of male and female traditional dancers. An important question is: why, amidst all the spotlight on fancy dancing, are the traditional forms still done? The answer is that through the mechanism of oral tradition, the significance of traditional dance has been instilled in generation after generation of Indian people. And because each new generation understands that traditional dances must be preserved not only for themselves but because such dances are a connection to a demonstration of spiritual beliefs, a demonstration of harmony with all life, or a depiction of particular events. That, after all, is how oral tradition works.

Joseph Marshall III

150

One hopes that many people of each generation learn about as many aspects of culture as possible. Learning one's native language is a key to learning about other aspects of culture. But if a singer of songs, for example, teaches his or her songs and passes on crucial knowledge about songs and their significance to ceremonies and spiritual beliefs *to at least one more person,* there is some hope that a particular tradition will endure for at least one more generation.

The conveyance of oral tradition to the written, audio, and visual record can serve a purpose also. But we must understand that the essence of a culture—or of a particular word, story, or ceremony—must also be preserved. Take, for example, one of the story lines from a past episode of the television series *Northern Exposure.*

In the episode a young Indian wrestles with the question of how to preserve the art of flute making. He finally understands that actually learning how to *make* a flute is far more meaningful than *filming the making* of a flute. That aspect of culture then lives on in him in many dimensions, instead of only one. He now not only knows how to make a flute with his own hands, he also knows which types of wood are preferred and why, and how to play the flute. Furthermore, once he learns how to play, he learns the songs.

Indian oral tradition is a very simple mechanism. It was intended to be so. There is strength in simplicity. Most people remember a strong, quiet voice better than the one which is shallow and strident. Oral tradition is that strong, quiet voice. It relies on patience and persistence. That is why it has survived to this day, wearing many faces and speaking many languages.

Voices in the Wind

Those voices from the past, coming on the winds of memory and riding on the strength of simple tradition can continue to speak to us. They connect us to what was and sometimes to what is.

I once heard a story about a group of Pawnee warriors making a raid into Lakota country, probably sometime after 1840 since in the story they and the Lakota had firearms. After a brief skirmish the Pawnee were repelled and chased back south toward the sand hill country in what is now Nebraska. Somewhere on a tree-covered ridge south of the Smoking Earth (Little White) River, they were entirely surrounded. A day-long fight ensued. Some Lakota were wounded and some of the Pawnee killed. Finally, the Pawnee surrendered. The Lakota took their horses and weapons and sent them back to their country on foot.

This story remained tucked away in my memory until the early 1980s when a survey crew, laying out the route to straighten a dangerous portion of U.S. Highway 16, uncovered evidence of human remains west of Mission, South Dakota. The evidence was significant enough for the South Dakota state archaeologist to investigate, and the result was a recommendation that the highway be rerouted around the site—a ridge some distance south of the Little White River. Although I am not unequivocally stating that the site is where the Pawnee in the story made a stand against my ancestors, it would be intriguing to learn if anyone else has heard the same or a similar story that might link the historical event to the site.

The message here is that oral tradition should not be offhandedly dismissed as unreliable or without foundation. It is as viable as any aspect of our past and contemporary cultures, viable as part of our identities as Indian peoples. It can transcend time itself and make a past event seem like it happened only yesterday. Or it can personify Iktomi and gently put someone in his moccasins, so to speak, to impart a quiet but necessary lesson.

Oral tradition is the wind which carries the voices of our loved ones from the past, whether over one generation or a hundred. We should listen to their voices and pass on their stories because they are our stories as well. After we have turned to dust, our stories shall endure and carry on the essence of what we are and were. For certain, someday we shall join all the other voices in the wind.

On Making a Bow

Winter is my favorite season. When the thin sliver of a new moon chases loneliness from the night sky, when breaths of four-leggeds and two-leggeds crystallize into floating mist, when snow crunches beneath paws, hooves, and feet, there is a renewed vibrancy to the relationship of life and death. When I see falling snow, it triggers genetic memories of nameless ancestors on snowshoes, with weapons in hand, enduring the cold to pursue shaggy bison fleeing laboriously through shoulder-high, blue-white drifts. Both hunter and hunted pursuing life, trying to hold death at bay. Sometimes the hunter is successful, sometimes the hunted.

The pursuit of life is the legacy we Indians or Native Americans have inherited from those who have inhabited this land before us. It matters not if that legacy does not exist as specific memories in our conscious awarenesses, because it flows in our blood. And because even if some of us will never learn to remember, some of us do.

For me, sojourns into the past can happen anytime but occur most often in the winter when I stand on a snow-swept plain. Likewise, anytime I pick up a

Lakota flatbow—especially one I have made with my own hands—I walk back into yesterday. Those are the ways I remember that legacy and how I celebrate it. Like winter, bows have come to represent, for me, the vibrant partnership of life and death.

A bow has two identities. One for what it is—a weapon—and the other for what it represents—life. The first identity is obvious, the second is very well hidden. To find it, one must learn to make a bow.

By simplest definition a bow is a thing, a noun, an artifact. It has width, depth, and length and is most easily perceived by sight and touch. It is a composite of several different materials which make it a whole—wood, sinew, and glue. That whole is further defined by its functioning parts—the back, belly, top limb, bottom limb, handle, string notches, and string. All of which adds up to potential energy that can be turned into kinetic energy, provided that craftmanship was sufficiently skillful to correctly adhere to proven design. That is a bow—simply defined, perhaps, but not a simple entity.

A bow is first and always thought of as a weapon. Even though a modern archer may use a particular bow for nothing but shooting at targets, that archer is still conscious on some level that the object in the hands is a weapon. A human's basic predatory nature automatically designates it as such, even if there is no specific awareness of its origins and atavistic uses.

One of the most basic definitions of a weapon is *a means by which one contends against another.* The use of the bow by the pre-European inhabitants of this continent certainly falls within the parameters of this definition. The Indian hunter surely contended or strived against hunger, cold, and nakedness to provide food, shelter, and clothing by using the bow to bring down small and large animals. The Indian warrior used it to contend against the encroachment of enemies who threatened life and territory.

Any weapon is perceived to be an instrument of pain and death. Bows and arrows of primitive North America certainly were. Yet that perception is of only one aspect. It is more fitting and accurate to say that the bows and arrows of the pre-European peoples of North America were instruments of *life and death*. This brings us to the question of what a bow represents.

The primitive bow is more than an instrument or a weapon, more than its obvious form, parts, and function. It is given substance, purpose, and spirit by different entities within the realm of physical existence: trees, four-leggeds, and two-leggeds. It is born of death and must cause death to provide life.

A bow begins its existence as a tree, and as animal hide, tendon, and hoof (and sometimes horn). In the northern Plains many tribes regarded chokecherry, ash, and oak as the best types of wood for bows. Elsewhere other tribes used vine maple, juniper, osage orange, hickory, black walnut, and a variety of other hardwoods. Rawhide from deer, antelope, elk, and bison was sometimes used as a backing applied with glue made by boiling hide scrapings and (ungulate) hooves. Sinew made from dried tendons was also sometimes used as bow backing and was the favorite material for the bowstring since it was extremely strong, although rawhide from small animals such as rabbits and squirrels, sliced into long, thin circular strips, also made

Joseph Marshall III

durable bowstrings. In short, all of the various components that make a bow were all part of a living organism. In order for them to become part of the bow, that organism, that life, had to die. This fact served to remind the maker that all things are connected in life and by death.

Death is a catalyst. It is that through which a transformation is made; consequently, it is never regarded only as an ending because it is also a beginning. When a bow is made, though the life of a tree, an antelope, or a deer may have ended, their flesh is changed into a new entity with both an old and a new identity. The new identity is the bow, given ability by the old identities, which are the strength and resiliency of wood, glue, and sinew. Anyone who builds a primitive bow, therefore, has in his or her hands an essential lesson on existence: that which comes after birth and that which comes after death. And finally, to respect the lives that were ended (so that the bow could be made) and to give them new meaning, the craftsperson strives to make the best bow that knowledge and skill can produce. This parallels the beliefs of many pre-European peoples that one should live one's life as well as possible in order to have a meaningful existence in the next life.

It is difficult to speak of bows without also speaking of arrows. It is a natural association. One can exist without the other, but neither can fulfill its purpose without the other. One gives additional meaning to the other within the parameters of relationship. This bond can even be considered a marriage. Indeed, in some marriage ceremonies (before Christianity came onto the scene) an elder would advise the couple to form a band "like the bow and arrow." In that bonding, the bow had to be strong, and the arrow had to be straight. If the bow was not strong, it did not matter how straight the arrow could fly. If the arrow was not straight, it did not matter how strong the bow was. Strength was necessary for the bow to send the arrow all the way to the target. It was necessary for the arrow to be straight so that it could fly true, without deviating one way or another.

The arrow went through the same transformation as the bow in the process of construction. It, too, was composed of once living entities that were given new purpose and meaning by the knowledge and skill of the maker. The shaft was either chokecherry, willow, or gooseberry (and several other) stalks. Fletching was feathers taken from such birds as ravens, turkeys, hawks, or sage hens. Points were made from stone such as chert, flint, or obsidian, which were themselves composed of once living organisms. Points and fletching were wrapped into place and onto the shaft with sinew. Therefore, the making of an arrow provided the same lessons about life and existence as the bow.

Bows and arrows were the primary weapons of hunters and warriors for many generations in primitive North America. A long slide into obsolescence began with the arrival of European firearms. Reservations brought the final, swift end to many hunter/warrior cultures—and with it the bow and arrow. Their disappearance also meant the loss of philosophies and beliefs surrounding their manufacture and use. Fortunately, like other aspects of Native American cultures disapproved of or forbidden by Euro-American

Joseph Marshall III

government and church policies, the knowledge and skills to make bows and arrows were quietly kept alive by a few individuals.

Native American bows and arrows are becoming popular again as physical and cultural artifacts because they have been suddenly "discovered" by practitioners of traditional and primitive archery. But while it may be possible to replicate the physical appearance of primitive Indian bows and arrows, it is difficult to recall the cultural and spiritual significance they once had. When and if that happens, the renaissance will be complete.

On the pre-European Plains of Turtle Island, or North America, every hunter/warrior knew the basics of making his own bows and arrows. There were two basic requirements important to production: materials and craftsmanship. The hunter/warrior had to know which woods were best for bows and arrows, where to find them, when to harvest them, and how to season or cure them. Once the material was properly seasoned, then he needed precise physical skills to measure, split, shave, bend, and otherwise work the wood. Furthermore, he needed to know the characteristics of each kind of wood. In addition, he had to know how to prepare rawhide, hide glue, and sinew as well as how to find, hand split, and trim feathers.

The Bow

I recall my grandfather's reply to a question about the first step in making a deerskin shirt. He said, "Get the deer." Likewise, the first step in making a bow was to find the right kind and size of tree. Familiarity with a given territory meant knowing where the appropriate-sized chokecherry, ash, and oak trees were. The tree was selected and cut, and that became a bow stave, about the size of a man's forearm and about shoulder height in length.

After the stave was cut to length, it was split in half and sometimes into fourths. Some bow makers left the bark on, and some peeled it. A few times during the drying process, the stave was put in water (a shallow inlet or the edge of a stream) and soaked for days and then air dried again. This, of course, was a summer chore, and it seemed to harden the wood even more. (To appreciate this process, observe the toughness of a piece of dried driftwood.)

Split bow staves were tied together in sort of a chain in the order they were harvested. The oldest stave, marked with a notch or a groove, was on the right, the next oldest to its left, and so on. So the stave on the extreme left was the newest and least seasoned. When the oldest stave was removed to make a bow, the next oldest was then marked. Several staves were kept on hand at all times, and five years was the minimum required seasoning time. Unless the situation warranted, a bow maker would rarely make a bow from anything less than a fully-seasoned stave. Although it was possible to make a bow from an unseasoned stave using a carefully managed bed of hardwood coals as the drying agent, a bow made in this manner usually was not as durable—in terms of longevity or service—as one that was slowly seasoned and occasionally soaked in water.

One other way to circumvent the long seasoning time was to look for wood that had been struck by lightning, especially ash. A tree felled by lightning was dried, seasoned, and hardened in the blink of an eye and proved to be especially flexible as well as durable.

When a bow maker chose a seasoned stave and began the process of handcrafting the bow, he first measured it to the proper length for the eventual owner and shooter—either the artisan himself or someone else. The length of the bow also depended on its intended use. After the acquisition of horses, bows used to hunt bison or used in warfare were usually shorter than those made for other uses. The Lakota, by and large, measured such bows from the ground to the small of the owner's back. Bows used to hunt anything from small game to antelope and deer were generally longer. Their length (also assessed by a Lakota method) was from the index finger of the outstretched arm (straight from the shoulder) in a straight line to the opposite hip bone.

After the stave was measured, the bow maker next marked out (usually with charcoal) the approximate dimensions of the bow. If the bark had not been previously peeled, it was removed at this juncture. The side to side width of the bow at the middle was usually two fingers wide, and at the ends about the size of a man's little finger. Thus, the bow was tapered from the middle to the ends.

The next step was to pare the stave down to the outline with a hand axe. Once that rough outline was achieved, the bow maker then began to shave (not carve or whittle) it down further with a smaller, straight-edged tool. He had to make certain that the belly or inside of the bow (the side toward the user when held in

On Making a Bow

the bow hand) was flat so that the limbs would flex readily when the bow was drawn. The outside or back of the bow (the side away from the user) was usually left in its naturally slightly curved (from side toside) configuration, although the bow maker made sure that all of the bark had been removed. During this part of the process, the bow maker would frequently test the bend of the bow over his knee by pulling the tips of the limbs carefully inward (toward himself). This was not to test the strength of the limbs but to visually assess the bend in each limb to ensure that it was flexing evenly or uniformly. Limbs that bent unevenly meant that the weaker was more stressed and would easily break if the imbalance was not corrected. Symmetry was not only aesthetically important but functionally necessary as well.

Watching my grandfather make a bow was unquestionably the best way for me to learn. Step-by-step instructions did not roll out of his mouth as he worked; instead he worked slowly and patiently answered questions. It was his answer to my very first question that I will always remember most vividly. When I saw him sizing an ash bow stave, I asked him what he was planning on doing. His reply was, "There is a bow inside of here, and I am going to help it come out."

The process, beginning with the paring of the rough outline to the preliminary testing of the bend of the limbs, could take from five to fifteen days, depending on the experience and skill of the bow maker and the amount of time devoted each day to the task. Older, more experienced craftsmen could make bows faster than younger men. Furthermore, the overall task of making a bow was not begun until

Joseph Marshall III

the artisan was in the right frame of mind and felt himself to be in balance.

For bow making, the circumstances in the life of the artisan needed to be good. He needed to feel good about his family, current events, and himself. If he did not, the artisan would not begin the task until balance was achieved in his life. Or he interrupted the process if something happened which upset the balance—such as the death of a relative or a close friend—and would not begin again until balance was restored. He avoided negative emotions such as envy, jealousy, and anger. The logic here was that the bow maker imparted his spirit to the bow. If his spirit was weak or out of balance, then the bow's spirit would be weak as well. It was not unusual for a man to work on a bow during a high point in his life, or begin after a positive or fortuitous event. The bow's balance and strength, then, came not only from the physical but also from the spiritual level.

An additional aspect of balance had to do with the bow's own relationship to the earth when it was still a living tree. When the tree was first cut, the bottom or end closest to the roots was marked. Throughout the construction process, the bow maker was careful to maintain the bow's vertical balance. Therefore, the bottom end of the bow was the one that had been the bottom of the young tree. At the point where he began testing the flex of the limbs, he cut one string notch in the top and two at the bottom. Older, experienced bow makers were quick to point out that a vertically inverted bow, thus one out of balance, would soon break. As a tree, it had received the flow of life

On Making a Bow

from one direction—upward from the earth. In order to maintain its spiritual connection to the earth as a bow, it needed that vertical balance.

Bows of the northern Plains tribes, especially the Lakota, were a single piece of hardwood. Once the bow maker was satisfied that the flex of the limbs was even, it was mostly finished. From this point he could decide to keep it unbacked, or to back it with a layer of rawhide or hamstring sinew. Either way, he had satisfied an important and basic requirement. With the string attached and the limbs drawn, the bow had to resemble the curvature and appearance of the thin sliver of a new moon. It was thickest in the middle, at the handle, and each limb tapered gracefully to a point. In this way the bow became a relative of the moon, and in some cultures was regarded as female and mother.

If the bow was to remain a simple piece of hardwood without a backing, the bow maker then rubbed its entire surface with an ungulate leg bone or an antler tine. This compressed and closed the wood's grain, increased its durability, and helped prevent cracking and breaking on the outside or back of the bow when it was drawn. Rubbing also gave the wood a glossy sheen and added some water repellency. Finishing touches after that might include a handle wrap of some type and, for hunting bows, a fringed wrap near the tips of each limb, which functioned as silencers.

Most of the bows made on the northern Plains were unbacked. It was much easier to leave them that way, relying on the proven tapered design and expert tillering of the limbs to prevent breakage. When bows were backed, rawhide was the most common material used.

Joseph Marshall III

Rawhide was the product of the animal hide in the tanning process that had been dehaired before oils and brains were rubbed in. To make backing for a bow, a long strip the width of the bow was cut, soaked in water, and then applied to the back or outside (the side away from the shooter) with hide glue. It was then allowed to dry for days before excess glue was scraped off and the dried rawhide was trimmed to the width of the bow. The only reason for rawhide backing was to prevent breaking. Since rawhide is an inert material, it did not add to the strength of the bow. Sinew was another matter.

Sinew for backing bows was taken from the hamstring tendon of ungulates such as antelope, deer, elk, and bison. Antelope tendon was the most desirable since antelope were the swiftest hoofed animals. Sinew was more difficult to apply to a bow than rawhide because it had to be glued on in fibrous strips no wider than about an eighth of an inch. The back of the bow was prepared by roughing the surface, and the sinew was soaked in tepid water until its fibers expanded or thickened. Next, the back of the bow was scored with hide glue. Then strips of sinew were dipped in glue and laid onto the bow surface lengthwise. Depending on the number of layers of sinew, this task could easily consume half a day or more. Finally, the bow was carefully hung from the lodge poles just below the smoke hole and allowed to dry for as long as an entire month.

As the sinew dried, it contracted; thus, a multilayered backing always reflexed the bow. When fully dried, the sinew not only prevented breakage, but it also increased the power or strength of the bow. Sinew-backed bows could cast arrows greater distances at a higher velocity and flatter trajectory than unbacked or rawhide-backed bows. Some bows used for bison hunting were so stout that it required a four-fingered hold to draw them.

Sinew was also the preferred material for bowstring. It was pulled apart into long, thread-sized strips. The strips were then intertwined by twisting or rolling them by hand over a curved surface, such as a man's thigh. Another method was to roll the strips between the palms. Length and overall thickness of the bowstring were achieved by adding fibers or strips until three different lengths—each from outstretched fingertip to outstretched fingertip—were made. The three portions were then twisted together with a loop braided into one end for the top notch of the bow. A slip loop was twisted into the bottom end for the two bottom notches of the bow and kept in place by pressure once the bow was tautly strung. Since bowstrings were susceptible to moisture, the hunter/warrior always carried spares.

It is difficult to say exactly when the bow first appeared on this continent. It is highly likely that it was developed here independently (as it did in other parts of the world) possibly at different times and different locations. In any case, by the time bows and arrows appeared, from fifteen hundred to six thousand years ago, the forerunners of this weapon had already been in existence for many generations, namely the atlatl (or spear thrower) dart and the bow drill fire starter. At some point it is probable that someone, more than

Joseph Marshall III

likely quite by accident, noticed the bow drill's ability to send its drill stick flying. Once that ability was tested and verified, it was only a matter of time before someone deduced that the atlatl dart could be reduced in size and length, since it already was essentially an arrow. That is my theory about the development of the primitive bow and arrow on Turtle Island.

The Arrow

The Pawnee and the Lakota along with several other tribes said that arrows must be as straight as the sun's rays shining down through cloud banks. That, of course, is as straight as straight can be. But that simple philosophy is based on hard reality. Any well-made bow is capable of sending an arrow, but accuracy depends most on the arrow. A straight arrow will follow a straight line of flight, affected eventually only by gravity. Of course, there is one other significant factor which also helps to determine accuracy—the release of the string and the arrow by the archer. Still, if the arrow is not as straight as straight can be, no other factor will matter.

Arrows were made from both softwood and hardwood stalks harvested mainly in winter. Stalks were cut just above the ground's surface. They needed to be without twists and bends, about an arm's length long and the width of a man's index finger with the bark still on.

The next task, after cutting, was to peel the bark, then hand-straighten the green stalks, and finally tie several together in a bundle. A bundle was often hung just below the smoke hole of a lodge, where the rising warm air helped the drying process. About every other day the stalks were taken down and hand-straightened again.

Although hardwoods made more durable arrows, more arrows were made from softwoods. They dried faster and were easier to straighten and work. Some arrow makers resoaked dried shafts in water (as was done with bow wood) during appropriate seasons and weather, of course. This practice not only helped to restraighten unusually stubborn shafts but also helped give them additional durability.

A fully-seasoned shaft was then cut to the proper length. One method of measurement used by the Lakota was from the elbow of the bent arm to the tip of the middle finger, plus the width of a hand. Then the process of sizing the shaft began.

Just as the bottom of the bow stave was the end closest to the roots of the tree, the nock end (the end placed on the string) of the arrow had to be the bottom end of the stalks as it grew. The point end (where the arrowhead was attached) had to be the end of the stalk that had been pointing up into the sky.

The raw stalk in its dried state has a natural taper. The upper end is narrower with a gradual increase in width to the root or bottom end. Most arrow makers preferred a uniform-sized, straight shaft, definitely in the interest of accuracy. There were two methods of producing an arrow shaft that was the same width from end to end, except for the string nock.

Both methods required the use of a sizer. The basic purpose of the sizer was to ensure a uniform width, but it could also be the tool used to achieve that

Joseph Marshall III

width. One kind of sizer was a hand-sized piece of sandstone with a straight, half-circle groove chipped into its middle. The shaft was worked through the groove until it had been shaved (sanded) down to the desired uniform width from end to end. Another kind of sizer was an object with a hole in it the size of the required shaft size. This kind of sizer could be a stone or an antler tine with a hole drilled in it, often attached to a wood handle. It helped the arrow maker to achieve uniform shaft width by compression rather than by sanding or shaving. One way to do this was to force the shaft through the hole little by little, starting at the narrower (or top) end. Another way was to use a length of antler tine with a half-circle groove in the middle. The arrow maker sat above the shaft, which lay perpendicular to him on a long, hardwood base. Then, with the long antler tine, he pressed down on the shaft, applying the pressure back and forth and occasionally rotating the shaft. Now and then he would check his progress by inserting the shaft into the sizer until it could slide easily through its entire length to the nock end.

These were not, by any means, the only methods of sizing arrow shafts, but they were the ones most often used by arrow makers among tribes on the northern Plains, especially the Lakota. Invariably, each craftsman added his own innovation to accelerate or facilitate the process. But all artisans understood that the steps up to this point were the most important, since a straight shaft of uniform size was essential to accuracy.

The next steps were making grooves or openings for the nock end and the arrowhead. The nock groove was usually made first. In sizing the shaft, the nock end (the bottom) was left wider, so much that it looked bulbous in comparison to the rest of the shaft. One reason for this was because it served as an aid when drawing the arrow. The easiest method for making the string nock was simply to cut away material until the V-shaped, open nock was achieved. A final step was tapering the entire nock end until it resembled a flower bud about to bloom. Some nocks were shallower than others, but its open configuration was essential to the rapid firing of arrows. It is much more difficult to quickly place an arrow with a narrow nock onto the string.

Another method of making nocks began with a narrow cut or slice into the middle of the bulbous end, obviously in the direction of the shaft. Then that end was thoroughly soaked in water until softened, after which it was pushed down onto V-shaped piece of hardwood (obviously carved to that shape.) The water-soaked end opened to fit the shape and was left to dry. After that, the nock end was tapered.

With either method, the bottom or middle of the nock opening had to be precisely in the middle of the shaft. Any deviation would, of course, affect accuracy.

The groove or opening for the arrowhead required no less precision, because the arrowhead had to be attached on a straight line in balance with the shaft. The middle of the very tip had to coincide with the middle of the shaft. Since the early stone arrowheads were not all the same exact size at the base, the top end of each shaft was basically custom fitted to an arrowhead. That meant patience and careful carving and grooving until the fit was attained. The groove or opening had to be sufficiently deep enough so that the arrowhead, when slid in and held horizontally, would not fall out. After that, the top end around the groove was given a gradual taper to eliminate blunt or pronounced surfaces, thus reducing wind resistance.

The arrowhead was then glued in place and its base further attached to the shaft with sinew wrapping or lashing. The sinew wrappings were soaked lightly, often with saliva, just before the wrapping. The finished wrap was sometimes coated lightly with hide glue. With or without hide glue, once the sinew dried, some arrow makers added a coating of warm pine pitch, since it was an effective moisture barrier when dry, especially for arrows used in winter hunting in areas of heavy snowfall.

There was a difference between hunting arrows and war arrows, most notably in the manner in which arrowheads were attached. A hunting arrowhead was attached vertically to enable it to pass between the ribs of an animal such as elk, deer, or antelope. A war arrowhead was attached horizontally to pass between the ribs of a man. Since arrows spin in flight and the points do not remain vertical or horizontal, the most important aspect of such differentiation was psychological and spiritual. Each kind of arrow had a different and equally necessary purpose. Beyond that, some arrow makers made heavier arrows for hunting and lighter arrows for warfare. A heavier arrow had more penetrating power and thus speeded up the demise of the quarry. By contrast, a lighter arrow flew faster in a situation where speed often meant the difference between life and death.

Before the fletching was attached, the crest was painted on. In the area on the shaft beneath the feathers (anywhere from four to six inches long), the specific identifying mark of the owner was painted. The crest was usually a series of wide or thin rings painted around the shaft, sometimes accompanied by dots or hailstone marks. The colors most commonly used were blue, black, and red. A crest was in essence the signature of the hunter/warrior. In a communal buffalo hunt, the hunter's family looked for his arrows embedded in the carcasses of the fallen animals. (My crest is an inch-wide red band with a thin black border on each end.)

After the crest was painted, the fletching was made, which usually consisted of two hand-split feathers of any type. Goose and duck feathers were popular for arrows used in winter hunting because of their better resistance to moisture. The length of the fletching was arbitrary, varying from artisan to artisan, and anywhere from four to six inches long. Some were measured from the middle of the base of the hand to the tip of the thumb. Others were measured from the base of the hand to the line of the top joint of the index (middle) finger.

Both feathers had to have the same curvature, so the two halves of the same feather could not be used. Opposite curvature meant very erratic arrow flight. Some fletching was attached straight down the middle of the shaft. But someone at some point noticed that

Joseph Marshall III

attaching the fletching in accordance with its natural curve caused the arrow to spin in flight and, thereby, increase accuracy. After the base or bottom end of the fletching and the top or narrower end were bared to about a finger's width, the feathers were first glued on—but only at each end. Then they were wrapped with sinew in exactly the same way as the arrowhead. A final step was trimming the feathers so that each was the same height outward from the shaft. This was done with a hot ember, usually the end of a long, dry twig placed in the fire. If necessary, the burned ends were quickly rubbed with wet material.

At some point, either before or after the arrowhead and fletching were attached, a long lightning (zigzag) groove was pressed (not carved) into the length of the shaft on both sides. The popular belief today is that this was a "bloodline" or a mechanism which promoted or aided bleeding when an animal was shot. However, my grandfather's rationale for the lightning groove was twofold. First, on the more important level, it was a wish or a prayer for the arrow to have the speed and power of lightning. Secondly, he was absolutely convinced that the groove helped the shaft to remain straight. I definitely lean toward my grandfather's rationale.

The only significant later innovations in arrow design and manufacture were the use of three feathers for fletching and the iron arrowhead. Adaptation to iron arrowheads occurred after the arrival of European-made objects such as iron kettles, pots, and barrel hoops that could be melted down and poured into forms or cut with a cold chisel or flat file. But it is not as easy to ascertain when three-fletching first came into consistent use. Of course, among us Indians, the *when* is not as important as the innovation itself; the fact that it did happen is indescribably more important.

Two-fletching was popular for two immensely logical reasons. First, two feathers were easier to obtain than three. Second, two-fletching meant there was no up or down relative to how one nocked (loaded) the arrow on the string. Once the arrow was on the string, one feather would always be up and one would always be down. This enabled rapid nocking and, hence, rapid firing. The most accomplished Indian archers could nock and fire entirely by feel or touch, to the extent that they could launch anywhere from twelve to sixteen arrows in the span of thirty seconds.

A third feather on the shaft meant more work for the craftsman and slower shooting for the archer. Three feathers required different spacing because of the third feather, and since the up or cock feather had to be outward (away from the handle of the bow), it slowed the nocking and firing process. My theory is that three-fletched arrows were used predominantly for hunting because they provided more stability in flight. In most instances, the hunter was more deliberate when aiming and shooting at game because he wanted to be as accurate as possible. A missed opportunity meant that his family went hungry. Therefore, if he observed that three-fletched arrows increased his accuracy, he would make and use them because they improved his ability to provide for his family.

The mechanics of shooting bows and arrows differed from tribe to tribe and even from individual to

Joseph Marshall III

individual, influenced by bow style and length. There were various ways to hold the arrow on the string, all intended to enable good aiming and a smooth release.

Among the northern Plains tribes, and certainly among the Lakota, there was an interesting step in the process of shooting. Once the arrow was nocked onto the string and laid over the bow hand (which is essentially the shooting shelf), the archer lifted bow and arrow upward so that the arrow pointed toward the sky before it was brought down to bear on the target. Mechanically, this is a highly effective method in the process of sighting in on the target. But my grandfather said that pointing the arrow skyward had a more important purpose.

Before the shaft became an arrow, it was a living stalk growing upward from the earth and, like any tree or plant, received its life-giving nourishment and moisture from the ground and processed it upward toward the sky. As an arrow, the point or arrowhead was attached to the upward end. When it was lifted upward, the archer—if only for a heartbeat or two—realigned the arrow with those forces that had given it viability as a living thing. In a manner of speaking, the archer was praying for the arrow to have balance before he launched it toward the target. And that act itself was closing a circle. A living stalk had died to become an arrow, an instrument to bring death so that, from that death, life could be sustained for the hunter and his family.

The circle of life and death were certainly represented by bow and arrows, and the hunter/warrior was reminded of this fact each time he saw, touched, and used these weapons. But he further acknowledged this fact if he were successful in bringing down an animal.

On Making a Bow

After an animal had died, the hunter would usually leave an offering as a profound expression of his gratitude and indebtedness. Some hunters left small bundles of sage or tiny bags of tobacco (tobacco ties) or offered a drink of water so that the animal would never be thirsty in the next life. Others would leave tiny pieces of their own flesh (usually gouged from their upper arms), strands of their own hair, or drops of their own blood. Interestingly, the hunter had probably done the same thing when he had harvested the wood for his bow and arrows. It was another way to close the circle.

Today, there is a renewed interest in primitive bows and arrows in this country as part of the "sport" of archery. More and more people are attempting to handcraft their own archery equipment. But I find it interesting that while bows and arrows are constructed with natural materials, many are built to resemble the more modern designs of what is called "traditional archery." This practice, in my opinion, overlooks the essence if not the purity of what primitive archery once was. Thus, one may build a three-dimensional, functioning "primitive" artifact and still remain largely unaware of the atavistic philosophies and beliefs that are an essential part of it.

In this context, I am reminded of a group of Indian women on one of the western reservations who, a few years ago, attempted to revive an ancient quilling society. While they knew how to quill, no one could remember all of the songs that had to accompany certain ceremonies. Rather than speculate or make up new songs, they ceased their effort to revive the society, based on the logic that the essence of it was lost. Without

Joseph Marshall III

that, they felt, there was no real or true connection to the old times.

Similarly, primitive archery can never be truly reborn until all of the aspects of it which gave it essence are used or followed, including the correct, respectful ways to harvest natural materials, the use of actual primitive tools, and adherence to ancient designs.

There is nothing wrong with using modern materials and tools to build primitive-style bows and arrows. But there is an indescribable sense of satisfaction and communion when one can build bows and arrows entirely from natural materials using primitive methods and primitive tools. When you hold such objects in your hands, you realize that the only difference between them and those from a different age is time, and in such an instance, time becomes an inconsequential barrier. For some of us, it does not exist at all.

Making primitive bows and arrows by hand is a skill practiced by only a few people. The pulls and constraints of modern society dictate that it is easier to buy such things than to invest the time and effort to make one's own. To own a primitive weapon made by someone else, however, is not the same as making it yourself. Of course, many individuals shy away from the process because they lack the necessary knowledge and skills. Perhaps, on the surface, it would seem that building primitive bows and arrows is simply not necessary. Perhaps it seems that anything primitive has no place or purpose in this day and age. However, the fact is that through crafting such objects and attempting to understand the connection between man, nature, and spirit that results from making and using such objects, knowledge can be obtained and skills can be learned. And from that process can come awareness and wisdom—virtures that are never archaic or obsolete.

For me, crafting Lakota bows and arrows is necessary, not because I make a living doing so but because the process reminds me of the relationship of life and death. And it is a way to keep in touch with my grandfather.

The last bow I made was from a piece of osage orange—a gift from my friend Jay Massey of Girdwood, Alaska. As I sat under an elm with Elk (Casper) Mountain to the south, my tools ready and the billet clamped to my homemade shaving horse, I heard my grandfather's voice, saying "...there is a bow inside...you must carve away the wood that does not belong and let it come out." Eventually, from the wood emerged a fifty-two-inch Lakota-style flatbow that shoots hard and fast. But the process was just as important as the result.

The process of crafting the bow connects me to various aspects of the natural world from which the material came. Osage orange is a particularly hard and resilient wood, and it responds to the draw knife with a light, bell-like tone, almost as if it were singing. To me, that sound was the song of its life, telling of the breezes that had caressed its limbs and the birds that had nested in its branches, of the rains that quenched its thirst and the sustenance drawn from she who had given life to us both—Mother Earth. As I watched the bow taking shape, I was reminded that my own character and life were still being shaped by everyone and everything that touched me. Now finished, this bow is quite capable of sending an arrow swiftly each time I shoot it, thereby telling me that I should do all things to the best of my ability. Most of all, this primitive flatbow is to me the symbol of the circle that begins with birth and does not end with death.

Such knowledge and awareness, I believe, is just as relevant now as it ever was. Although there are other ways in which such knowledge can be attained, I believe that those who learn to handcraft primitive bows and arrows gain more than just a physical skill. They have a unique opportunity to participate in the vibrant relationship of life and death.

One could do far worse than make a bow.

The next bow I build will belong to my son who never quite made it into this world. After sixteen weeks in his mother's womb, he changed his mind or was called back. If he had come, I know he would have loved bows and arrows, much like one of his older brothers does. The bow I make for him will always have a place in our home, just as he will always have a special place in his parents' hearts. And each time I see hunters on snowshoes running in the deep, blue-white snow in pursuit of life, he will be one of them—with a bow in his hands—joyfully participating in the vibrant dance of life and death.

Standing Bear and the Mountain Men

All of the interaction of the past five hundred
years between the Europeans and their decendants
and the previous inhabitants of this continent is
too often conveniently condensed into the phrase
"clash of cultures." Although there certainly were
clashes or conflicts, they were not the only avenue
of interaction. Nor were they the only determining
factors which shaped our collective history, in spite of
the fact that Europeans and later Euro-Americans
readily turned to conflict, or the threat of conflict, in
their imperialistic rush over this land. There was
(and still is) also another force operating that is part
of the less aggressive side of human nature—
acculturation. This force is, I believe, more powerful
than *assimilation.*

Acculturation is intercultural borrowing
between diverse groups of peoples, often resulting in
new and blended patterns. It is the process by which
one acquires or becomes familiar with the culture of
another society. Assimilation, on the other hand,
means to absorb, or to make similar.

Both Native Americans and Europeans were and are acculturated to one another as a consequence of their interactions within the parameters of common physical existence on this continent, since the basic requirement is that the interactive groups are different from one another. Nevertheless, from the beginnings of that relationship, there existed the European desire and drive to assimilate the Indian, that is, to make the Indian more acceptable by making him more like the European. Assimilation was at the core of white missionary zeal to convert Native Americans from their "heathen" and "pagan" beliefs to Christianity. It was the reason that the United States government established institutions such as the Carlisle Indian School in Pennsylvania—to divest Native American students of their native cultures and imbue them with another. Assimilation was the goal when the Bureau of Indian Affairs in the 1950s and 1960s placed Native American families in large cities as part of the "Relocation Program"; though ostensibly done to provide employment and teach the "work" ethic, but the real goal was to immerse those families in the mainstream society to wash off what might be left of their native cultures. However, such attempts at assimilation failed to eradicate all aspects of Native American cultures simply because it is human nature to resist forced change.

Nevertheless, today the notion of assimilation remains a factor. There is still a viable and measurable feeling among some Euro-Americans that Native Americans would be "better off" in the mainstream of American life. Better off forsaking their ethnic identities, languages, values, traditions, spiritual beliefs, and (of course) what remains of their lands and jumping into the melting pot. There are still moments when a cry to terminate reservations resounds through the halls of Congress, forcing Indians to remind the national conscience that assimilation did not work and will not work under any guise, including termination.

Throughout the interaction and machinations of the last five hundred years, Indian identity has felt the influences of acculturation and assimilation and has changed as a consequence. But the most important result is that Indian identity—wearing many faces and wrapped in many cultures—still remains. And I believe it is necessary for each generation of Indians to learn their identities by examining the processes that have created it and continue to create it. Acculturation has been part of that process—a process that bears more scrutiny.

Acculturation is a significant factor in the continuing interaction between Native Americans and Euro-Americans. It occurs with each succeeding generation because it could not and cannot destroy the core aspects of either culture. A meteoric chapter in western American history provides an interesting case study and offers a lesson that is timely.

A compelling saga in the human history of this continent is that of the mountain man—not simply because of the mountain men but because of the process that created the type. When we turn the pages of history, it seems the mountain men suddenly emerged without any prototype. But the lifestyle of the mountain man was a product of acculturation and not a sudden aberation.

Joseph Marshall III

The label "mountain man" conjures up images of a breed of lonely white men noted for a self-sufficient lifestyle—a breed that found a niche somewhere between the natural environment and accepted Euro-American society of the time. Some notable mountain men were James Beckwourth, Jim Bridger, John Johnston, and J. F. "White Eye" Andersen. Most mountain men were fur trappers and traders, plying their trade in the Rocky Mountains. Some gained notoriety as "Indian fighters" and as scouts for the United States Army or as guides for immigrant trains heading west.

In terms of the entire span of North American history, the era of the mountain man was brief—from the beginning of the nineteenth century to its latter decades. We lament its passing and seem to totally ignore what its formative influences might have been. Two of those influences were European economics and Indian cultures.

The fur trade was the largest and most extensive economic activity instigated by the Europeans prior to 1900. It involved many people, many diverse ethnic groups, and much of the North American continent north of Mexico. More than any other activity, it contributed to extensive European exploration of this continent and caused extensive and intensive contact between Europeans and Indians. During its initial stages, some Europeans realized that the fastest way to procure furs to fill the demands from Europe was by using the Indian—that is, by using his geographic and topographic knowledge, his skills as a hunter and trapper, and his ability to survive in the natural environment. The Indian provided his knowledge and skills in return for kettles, paints, knives, cloth, firearms, and (unfortunately) liquor.

A consequence of this economic relationship was the human interaction and the subsequent effect both cultures had on each other. The European was learning how to hunt, trap, and live off the land; he was also gaining an insight into the less tangible aspects of Indian cultures—values, beliefs, and spiritualism. By the same token, the Indian was exposed to ideas, ways, artifacts, and philosophies different from his own. There could not have been a more natural avenue for acculturation than the fur trade.

The movement of the fur trade westward coincided with the emergence of the mountain man as we are most familiar with him—the solitary epitome of self-reliance and independence. But the specific knowledge and skills that actuated those characteristics were a result of acculturaltion to Indian lifestyles.

Among the early Europeans there were many approaches to interacting with the prior inhabitants of North America. Some were harsh, and some were not. The French learned early that the path to rapid accumulation of furs was the one of least resistance. And that meant adopting a lifestyle compatible with that of the Indian. (This philosophy did not, however, prevent the French from making war on some Indian tribes and now and then emulating the heavy-handed tactics of their English, Spanish, and Russian counterparts.)

That path of least resistance provided opportunities for Europeans to learn firsthand from Indians with whom they lived and worked. And somewhere in that process a significant number of

Joseph Marshall III

Europeans—French or otherwise—learned skills in basic survival, hunting, tracking, and trapping. Further, such close association with Indians was the best way for Europeans to obtain a basic understanding of Indian societies and values. Thus, the independent, self-reliant lifestyle of the mountain man was learned from Indians and based on Indian cultures. But it would be wrong to assume that mountain men necessarily became Indian, though in some instances their immersion in Indian cultures was so strong that it led to self-imposed assimilation. For the most part they adapted and used aspects of Indian cultures that were appealing or useful, from clothing to philosophy.

Many of the individuals who adopted the lifestyle of the mountain man were running away from their own society and culture. It is likely that the effect of an Indian culture on those individuals was very profound, perhaps to the point that their primary societal and cultural foundations were significantly altered. For such individuals the lifestyle of the mountain man was merely a stop on the way to becoming part of an Indian community and culture. But that immersion—or absorption—did not force expatriation or separation from any aspect of a previous lifestyle or community. Furthermore, it happened without Indian scorn, self-serving Indian ethnocentric rationale, or trauma. And a mountain man was free to return to his previous lifestyle anytime he chose.

The foregoing is only one end of the sprectrum of the influence of Indian cultures on the mountain men. There were, of course, mountain men who had little more than an economic relationship with Indian tribes. There were also those who were in conflict with one tribe while having an amicable arrangement with another. Moreover, there were mountain men who adopted an Indian lifestyle but still maintained a sense of white racial superiority. However, despite the spectrum of interrelationship and influence, we should not overlook the fact that acculturation was the process and the result. The era of the mountain man is a success story of acculturation; by contrast, the process of assimilation had no success stories.

Once Euro-American imperialism had taken most of the basis for many Indian cultures and identities—the land—there seemed to be no alternative but for Indians to stop being Indian. Assimilation was the obvious answer to the "Indian problem" for the United States government. It was also the most morally convenient. Indians becoming "white" was, at the same time, an invalidation of their own cultures and identities and a justification of Euro-American imperialism, ethnocentrism, and "manifest destiny." In the case of Standing Bear of the Ponca Tribe, the question of assimilation became the key to clarification of his legal status as a person within the terms of the Fourteenth Amendment to the United States Constitution. Without that, the ruling by Judge Elmer Dundy of the United States District Court for Nebraska in the case known as *Standing Bear v. Crook*, made on May 12, 1879, might well have been different.

Standing Bear v. Crook is regarded as a significant victory for Indian people as a whole because Judge Dundy ruled "that an *Indian* is a PERSON within the meaning of the laws of the United States." But he also ruled "that the Indians possess the inherent right of expatriation as well as the more fortunate white race. In other words Judge Dundy saw Indians as persons so long as they separated themselves from that which prevented them from being such—their Indian identity. In order to understand that, it is necessary to know the whole story of Standing Bear and his Ponca Tribe.

The Ponca, who never numbered more than a thousand, signed a treaty with the United States government in 1858 and accepted a reservation near the confluence of the Missouri and Niobrara rivers. There they hoped to live in peace while maintaining their agrarian lifestyle as they slowly acculturated themselves to the ways of the Euro-Americans. By 1868, according to white observers, the Ponca were making good progress in "becoming civilized." That year their reservation was inadvertently included in a vast tract of land set aside for the Sioux by the terms of the Fort Laramie Treaty. This oversight turned out to be the beginning of an ordeal which finally ended in 1879.

A group of whites purporting to represent the United States government came to the Ponca Reservation in 1876 saying that an order had been issued for removal of the tribe to Indian Territory in Oklahoma. The Ponca reminded the government that, according to their treaty, they could not be removed from their lands without their consent. Whereupon the "government representatives" countered with an offer to let some of the Ponca leaders see the Indian Territory themselves first. If they did not like the new land, they would not have to move. After some consultation, ten men decided to make the trip south.

Standing Bear and the Mountain Men

Once in Indian Territory, the ten Ponca leaders decided against leaving their reservation. The government's men then took a different tact, saying that the Ponca *must* trade their reservation land for land in Indian Territory. There was no longer a pretext of choice for the Indians. Then after the Ponca steadfastly refused, the government's representaives left them stranded in Indian Territory with no money and no provisions.

It took about sixty days for the men to walk back to the Omaha Reservation in eastern Nebraska. It was winter and they had to sleep out in the open, except for a few nights when they managed to find shelter in haystacks. Eventually, they returned to their own reservation, only to be harassed again by the people who had taken them to Oklahoma. Several months later, the Ponca agreed under duress to move to Indian Territory.

In Oklahoma, the Ponca knew little else but hunger and sickness. According to Standing Bear's own words, "There were dead in every family." Finally on the night of January 2, 1879, he and twenty-eight others fled north.

Ten weeks later, the twenty-nine Ponca finally made it to the Omaha Reservation, where their friends, the Omaha, took them in. The Ponca were hard at work plowing and planting crops when word reached them that they were to be arrested and returned to Indian Territory. On March 23, 1879, they were arrested by a United States Army detachment and taken to Fort Omaha, Nebraska, and detained.

The Ponca protested their detention at Fort Omaha, and word of their predicament reached Thomas H. Tibbles editor-in-chief of the *Omaha Daily Herald.*

Joseph Marshall III

188

After meeting with the Ponca, Tibbles came to their aid and enlisted the help of two lawyers. It is interesting that from the beginning of this case much was made about the degree to which this particular group of Ponca were "civilized." The petition read in part:

> that your complainants [referring to the Ponca] have made great advancements in civilization, and at the time of the arrest and imprisonment of your complainants, some of them were actually engaged in agriculture, and others were making preparations for immediate agricultural labors, and were supporting themselves by their own labors, and no one of these complainants, was receiving or asking support of the government of the United States.

Standing Bear's case went to trial on April 30, 1879, and lasted two days. On May 12, 1879, in a nearly three thousand-word opinion, Judge Dundy gave his ruling, whereby "Standing Bear became a person." Judge Dundy based his decision on Standing Bear's apparently voluntary severance from his own tribe and culture. In the opening paragraph he states:

> On the one side we have a few of the remnants of a once numerous and powerful, but now weak, insignificant, unlettered and generally despised race. On the other, we have the representatives of one of the most powerful, most enlightened, and most christianized

nations of modern times. On the one side we
have the representatives of this wasted race
coming into this national tribunal of ours
asking for justice and liberty to enable them
to adopt our boasted civilization and to pursue
the arts of peace, which have made us great
and happy as a nation.

Further into the opinion, Judge Dundy again
makes a substantial reference to the Ponca expatriation
and voluntary assimilation:

The petition alleges in substance that the
relators are Indians who have formerly
belonged to the Ponca Tribe of Indians,
now located in Indian Territory; that they
had some time previously withdrawn from
the tribe and completely severed their
tribal relations therewith, and had adopted
the general habits of the whites, and were
then endeavoring to maintain themselves
by their own exertions.

Judge Dundy's last reference to assimilation
and expatriation is made in direct reference to Standing
Bear himself:

He also states that he informed the agent of
their [the twenty-nine Poncas led by Standing
Bear] final purpose to leave, never to return,
and that he and his followers had finally, fully,
and forever severed his and their connection

Joseph Marshall III

190

with the Ponca tribe of Indians, and to cut
loose from the government, go to work,
become self-sustaining, and adopt the habits
and customs of a higher civilization.

And in reference to Standing Bear and his wife's
desire to bury the bones of their dead son in the earth
of their ancestral homeland though he had died in
Indian Territory, Judge Dundy stated:

Such instances of parental affection, and such
love of home and native land may be *heathen* in
origin, but it seems to me that they are not
unlike *christian* in principle.

Standing Bear's victory was important because
he and his followers were released from detention and
could not be removed to Indian Territory against their
will. But it was also important in the basic sense that
Indians were deemed to have the same legal standing as
any other people within the framework of the American
judicial system. However, Judge Dundy's ruling is based
substantially on the expatriation of Standing Bear (and
his followers) as a Ponca and his apparent willingness to
"elevate" himself to the "civilized" status of a white
person. One wonders what the ruling might have been
had Standing Bear kept firmly to his Ponca identity and
refused to embrace the tenets of that "higher
civilization," and had stated that he and his kind were
persons long before the world ever heard of the United
States of America. I doubt that the outcome would have
been the same in that instance. For the past five

Standing Bear and the Mountain Men

hundred years, assimilation has been popularly regarded as the answer to the "Indian problem," and nowhere is there a better testament to that belief than in Judge Dundy's ruling making Standing Bear "a person."

We Indians or Native Americans are identified and defined biologically, ethnologically, and legally. Identifying and defining us has been often more of a problem for non-Indians than it has been for us. But identity is far more than the labeling of a group of people. It is also, and more importantly, the sense that an individual has of himself or herself. Without a realistic, individual awareness of what one is ethnically, there can be no contribution to a community or group identity. Then the label of "Indian," "Native American," "Lakota," or "Ponca," or any other specific tribal name is only a veneer.

Obviously, much has happened to Indian tribes and individuals to weaken our basic sense of identity. Both acculturation and assimilation have been and are factors—the latter having done the most damage. One of the more popular theses to emerge from the discussion of Indian identity is the problem of "the Indian in two worlds": the non-Indian premise that Indians would have difficulty being Indians in a white society. But the problem has not so much been being in two worlds as it has been the expectation that we must sever all ties from the natural core of our identities— our "Indianness." Such an expectation is rooted in two equally false premises—first is that Indians are not as good as whites morally, physically, intellectually, or culturally; the second is that by shedding "Indianness" and striving to become like whites Indians are

Joseph Marshall III

automatically elevated to a higher status. Operating from such false premises, many Euro-Americans could not (and cannot) understand why Indians resisted assimilation, since we Indians would be changing ourselves into something better. The realities of that change are much more complex than this simplistic solution to the wrong problem.

Assimilation, the policy applied by American society to the "Indian problem," has failed because it was an approach designed to enable white Americans to feel more comfortable with Indians by making them facsimilies of "the representatives of one of the most powerful, most enlightened, and most christianized nations of modern times." It was not designed or applied in a manner that would enable Indians to find their own place in a different society. The prevailing Euro-American attitude at the time the policy of assimilation was intensively applied on a large scale—from the late 1800s to the 1960s—is summed up in the words of Henry Pratt, Superintendent of Carlisle Indian School in Carlisle, Pennsylvania, established in 1879 to house and educate Indian students: "...kill the Indian and save the man."

The policy and process of assimilation, then, were established and enforced so Euro-Americans could identify with the *man* once the *Indian* was destroyed. It was a policy and a process which was generally supported by white American society and reached into the core of Indian societies and cultures as well as individual lives.

Sadly and realistically, assimilation did and does have an impact to the extent that Indian cultures—languages, values, spiritual beliefs and practices, customs, lifestyles, land base, and sovereignty—have been altered. But it could not destroy all Indian cultures or all aspects of each culture, simply because it is a basic *human* reaction to resist when the defining aspects of one's humanity and identity are assaulted. As one old man from my reservation said about his experiences at a Jesuit boarding school, "They didn't let us talk Lakota out loud to each other, so we would whisper. But even so, some of us got caught and paddled. They [the Jesuits who ran the school] were tough and sneaky, but they couldn't stop us from thinking in Lakota."

Another example of how the notion of assimilation was arrogantly applied and how it affected individuals comes from my own family. About 1920 my maternal grandmother and her younger sister inherited land after their father had died. When they arrived at the Rosebud Agency (on the Rosebud Sioux Indian Reservation in South Dakota), the white Bureau of Indian Affairs employee who helped them with the paperwork necessary to record them as the new owners changed their first names on the spot. Although each of them already had a Euro-American or "Christian" first name, one became Fannie and the other became Annie. Soon afterwards Fannie died of Spanish influenza, but my grandmother Nellie was known as Annie until she died in 1984. Those relatives and friends who knew that her name had been changed continued to refer to her as Nellie throughout her life; but because of someone's fleeting act of self-righteous ethnocentrism,

Joseph Marshall III

her legal name became Annie Nellie Good Voice Eagle (and Two Hawk after she married my grandfather). However, my grandmother took the change in stride and never allowed it to affect her sense of self. Indeed, I learned the story of the name change from my mother and not from my grandmother.

Reservations, although synonymous with only Indians, are a direct result of Euro-American thinking or, more to the point, a Euro-American inability or unwillingness to coexist with Indians. An obvious solution to this lack of ability to coexist with Indians was to locate Indians as far as possible from Euro-American society, out of the way of "progress."

The concept of reservations, the setting aside of specific, limited tracts of land for Indians, originated in the Euro-American colonial period. In the 1820s, the idea of a permanent Indian homeland west of the Mississippi River found favor with some tribes tired of fighting with whites. By the 1830s the Andrew Jackson administration was calling it the Indian Territory. And by the middle of that decade, the federal government was given the right to quarantine Indians for the purpose of "civilizing." By the mid-1850s the Indian Territory comprised most of Oklahoma and parts of Kansas and Nebraska. Over time, the land base of the Territory was diminished by about seventy percent, but the concept of reservations remained intact. Today, there are over 380 reservations. Just over twenty are state reservations and the rest are federal.

In the 1870s and 1880s, since there were boundaries to reservations that imposed definite physical limits, Indians were turned literally into captive audiences for the purveyors of assimilation. The trauma of losing an inherent lifestyle was exacerbated by the imposition of another. For the Plains tribes this meant the end of the free-roaming, nomadic, hunting lifestyle which had been in a slow and painful demise for much of the nineteenth century. In connection with that particular lifestyle, reservations meant the end of one societal role and the affirmation, by pain of necessity, of another.

The image of the Plains Indian lifestyle (of all Indians for most non-Indian Americans) is the male Indian bedecked in feathers and mounted on a horse. But such an image represents only half of traditional Plains societies. The other half was female and, though less flamboyant and far less visible to white male historians, was no less important.

While the male filled the roles of hunter and warrior, or provider and protector, the female was the nurturer and the focal point of the family. Mothers and grandmothers were the primary influence on both male and female children in the critical formative years until about the age of five and six. There was an understanding among some tribes that while boys might acquire the skills to be hunters and warriors from fathers, uncles, and grandfathers, they learned courage from their mothers and grandmothers.

Reservations ended the need for hunters and warriors. The United States government promised annuities and to teach Indian men to be farmers; and, of course, there was no more warfare. A societal role which had existed for thousands of years and one preordained for boys before birth was rendered obsolete

Joseph Marshall III

in one fell swoop. Its existence had given meaning and purpose to generation after generation of males while helping to ensure societal and cultural survival. Its obsolescence became the vortex of forced change and turmoil. On the whole, Euro-Americans expected Indians to change lifestyles and values in much the same way a person changes one suit of clothes for another, failing to realize that divestiture of a culture that was reaffirmed by many generations for thousands of years cannot happen in one generation, or in two or three. Furthermore, the elimination of half of a society's basic reason for existence was the foundation for problems still plaguing Plains Indian peoples today, while at the same time placing an unexpected burden for the survival of entire societies on the other half of the society—in this case women.

Though the traditional role of hunters and warriors has no practical application (as opposed to philosophical) in modern Indian societies, the fact that Indian societies and cultures still exist is solid proof that Indian women were more than equal to the challenge given them by the invasive and pervasive policies of assimilation. The only change in their traditional role as nurturers and comforters and as the focal point of family, once reservations were established, was that it became the best hope for cultural survival; with the advent of reservation life, the role of women as examples of courage became essential to the survival of culture.

When the male sense of identity took a nearly fatal blow, it was Indian women who held Indian families, communities, societies, and cultures together during the most traumatic, widespread upheaval ever experienced by their people. This is not to say that Indian men did nothing to contribute to the general welfare. But the dysfunction brought on by the sudden loss of purpose and identity would have had a far more devastating impact if women had not kept to their milleniums-old role of being the mainstays for family. The reservation era made that role even more valuable and necessary, and thus it remains. Both of my grandfathers were strong individuals, but a significant portion of that strength was enabled or provided by my grandmothers. My parents raised ten children, uprooting and moving them several times because of employment considerations while seeing more than their share of difficult economic times. It was my mother who kept the family together and kept the sense of family intact through the most difficult times. (My father would be the first to agree.) This kind of role fulfillment continues to be the strongest aspect of Indian families, both on and off the reservation. It is one aspect of Indian cultures that assimilation could not alter or destroy. And it has been our best defense against new and difficult problems brought on by the transition from traditional lifestyles.

One of those problems is alcoholism, among others such as heart disease and diabetes. Those who treat and work with alcoholics in any segment of modern American society are quick to point out that low self-esteem is always one of the causes. Can there be a more certain basis for low self-esteem than the loss of one's reason for being? The realization that one's place and purpose within a society had suddenly ceased to

Joseph Marshall III

exist due to circumstances entirely beyond one's control would certainly leave a hole in one's life, filled all too quickly with confusion, self-doubt, and self-pity. And for Indian men after three or four generations, no sense of place, purpose, and identity as meaningful as that of the traditional role of hunter/warrior has yet emerged. Alcoholism continues to be a significant and tragic problem among Indians, and part of the solution to it certainly involves the development of a solid sense of identity, place, and purpose within one's family, community, and society. In my opinion, the problem continues to be exacerbated by the attitudes and influences of assimilation that still exist and that have fostered inept attempts by the federal government to "mainstream" Indians. One of those attempts was the BIA's Employment Assistance Program, also known as "Relocation."

In the 1950s and 1960s, the BIA implemented a poorly planned program to relocate Indian families from reservations into urban areas and find employment for the head of the family. In some cases jobs did not materialize as promised, and in nearly all cases the Indian families were not sufficiently prepared for life in a city. In too many instances the housing and living conditions were no better than what they had left behind, and sometimes they were worse. Due to such unexpected circumstances—mainly because the BIA did not adequately inform Indian families about urban life—most of the families who participated in the program returned to the more familiar and less terrifying setting of the reservations. Although some Indian families were fortunate to find themselves in good circumstances relative to employment and housing, and some persevered and made a living and a life for themselves in white urban America in spite of the BIA's ineptitude, insensitivity, and poor planning, these families were the exception rather than the rule. The Relocation program was a dismal failure as a vehicle for assimilation for this reason: there was still the expectation that its participants should give up their "Indianness" and become white in every way possible. Perhaps if the program had been structured to help Indians succeed as Indians in any setting, it might have been effective.

It is interesting to note that according to recent statistics, sixty percent of all Indians now live off-reservation. I suspect that most of them left by choice, because they felt it was necessary. I know that a decision to leave the reservation can be a difficult one, and the practical reasons for it are based mainly on opportunities for education, work, or career. But there is also a less obvious reason, one not always verbalized—*the challenge to exist and function in a non-Indian environment.*

Living in a non-Indian environment is always frightening but not always a deterrent to achievement, especially for those who realize that it is not necessary to give up their "Indianness" to do so. In order to succeed in a non-Indian environment, one must realize that this can be achieved by relying on Indian attributes and values. Such attributes and values can enable individuals and families to remain strong and intact, rather than trying to be non-Indians and thereby diminishing themselves. To put it another way, acculturation is preferable to assimilation. Furthermore,

Joseph Marshall III

it is possible for acculturation to have a positive impact on aspects of contemporary Indian life—as has been the case recently in education.

One of the most significant recent changes in Indian culture has been the establishment of Indian colleges—colleges founded by Indians, primarily for Indians, and located on reservations. The Navajo Community College in Arizona was the first of these to be established in 1968. On the Plains, Oglala Lakota College was founded in 1970 on the Pine Ridge Reservation and Sinte Gleska College in 1971 on the Rosebud Reservation. There are now a total of twenty-nine such institutions—all operated by Indian presidents, administrators, and Indian boards of directors or regents. These colleges were established to meet two basic needs: to provide reservation students with a releveant curricululm to enable them to function and compete in mainstream American society, and to help preserve Indian languages and cultures. These institutions are examples of the positive impact of acculturation and one of the best examples of the Indian ability to adapt to change, as we have been doing on this continent for tens of thousands of years.

In the past twenty years or more, Indians have also formed organizations such as the Coalition of Indian Controlled School Boards, the National Indian Education Association (along with several state Indian education associations), the American Indian Higher Education Consortium, and the American Indian Scholarship Fund. Furthermore, under the auspices of the 1975 Indian Self-Determination and Education Assistance Act (PL 93-638), many elementary and secondary schools formerly operated by the Bureau of Indian Affairs are now run by Indian school boards; and on at least one reservation in South Dakota, the tribal education code exceeds that of state requirements. All of these important steps have been taken because Indians see education as a key to the survival of Indians and their cultures, provided that the process is not divorced from Indian values and includes relevant curriculum, Indian teachers, Indian administrators, and input from Indian communities. Indians have decided that education can be given an Indian identity and still be an integral part of the American system of education—but not because non-Indians told us it was a way to become like them. Again, acculturation—based on experience, assessment, and choices—is at the core of this particular development

Indians have long realized that acculturation is preferable to assimilation. At one of the Fort Laramie treaty councils in the 1860s, one of the white peace commissioners raised the prospect that Indians would eventually have to give up their old ways and live like whites. An old Lakota man responded by saying that the whites should give them a thousand white women. The peace commissioners were, of course, grievously insulted at the prospect of white women cohabitating with Indian males. They did not know that in the Lakota culture the children belonged to the mother. Therefore, if the Lakota were to learn to live like whites, the most sensible and painless way would be to learn from a white mother to whom they would belong.

It is a basic human instinct to cling desperately to anything that someone else is trying to take. For us

Joseph Marshall III

Indians it was land, freedom, and culture. Hence, our identity. We have not lost it all, but neither have we been unaffected. We have been changed by both assimilation and acculturation, by what we have lost and by what we have adapted to or added. What remains and what has resulted is still Indian, and that is the basis for our humanity and our ethnicity—our identity. It is what we can offer to American society and to the world. But it must be accepted as is, seen for its own virtues and its own faults, not molded to fit someone else's pleasure or comfort. With such acceptance will come the realization that we Indians are a part of the mainstream of American life and the world community of cultures, either on the reservation or off.

I am proud to be "Indian" or "Native American" or "American Indian" because of the association with many unique pre-European cultures and peoples both ancient and contemporary throughout this country and continent. I am prouder of being "Sioux" because that label identifies my tribal nation and the Plains culture of which we are part. I am proudest of being "Lakota" because that label represents the dialect of the parent language I speak. It is the ethnic foundation for what I am, and it is the basis for who I am as a person.

What and who I am was shaped, affected, and forged by many people on both sides of the interaction of cultures, and thus by the acculturative and assimilative avenues of that interaction. From my father's side of the family are the French names of Marshall (probably originally Marichale) and Roubideaux, as well as Lakota names like Blunt Arrow. From my mother's side are such names as Two Hawk,

Good Voice Eagle, White Tail Feather, and Uses Cane. My family, like every other Indian family, has known the pain of assimilation and the benefit of acculturation. Our ancestors are a significant part of what has shaped who we are and offer us the lessons of why we are who we are.

Finally, we must not overlook the lessons of the past embodied in the Judge Dundys, the Standing Bears, and the mountain men. And for those of us who are Indian in any sense or in every sense, the most important lesson is that we can adapt, and even change to some extent, and still be Indian.

Joseph Marshall III

Journey to Altai

In September of 1994 I traveled to Barnaul, in Siberia, Russia. It was a learning experience, as all new adventures are. However, in another sense it meant a reconnection to heritage.

The journey was the result of an invitation to participate in an international conference on cross-cultural education in Barnaul, sent in May by Maria Obnarskaya of the organizing committee through Dr. Gretchen Ronnow of the Division of Humanities at Wayne State College in Wayne, Nebraska. After receiving the letter containing this intriguing offer, I stared for several minutes at the letterhead printed in Russian in the Cyrillic alphabet. Fortunately, the body of the letters from the Barnaul State Pedagogical University was in English. That invitation turned out to be the catalyst for enlightenment as well as reconnection.

Following several impatient minutes of finger skating over a world map, I located Barnaul in the Altai Territory, a region of Siberia, at about eighty-four degrees east longitude and fifty-four degrees north latitude. It was on the Ob River, roughly in the middle of what is now the Russian Federation, five or six hundred miles west of the largest freshwater lake on the planet—Lake Baikal. (What's a hundred miles to a country with twelve time zones?) To the southeast lay Mongolia and to the south was China.

The names in that region—Russia, Mongolia, and China—evoked images of mystery and exoticism. But the visions evoked of Siberia were a collage of darker and more difficult images connected to words like cold and exile and wasteland. However, in direct contrast to this, Dr. Ronnow had described her trips to Barnaul to teach summer-session English courses in terms of gentle people, beautiful landscapes, exhilarating hikes in the Gorno-Altai Mountains. Staring at the map, which showed Siberia as easily one-half of Russia, I was reminded that someone in the 1800s had called the Great Plains of North America "the Great American Desert" the same Great Plains my maternal grandfather spoke of in reverent phrases. I knew for a fact that the Plains that I loved were not a desert. Perhaps, I conceded, I should reserve judgment until after my first visit to Siberia.

Even before I had placed one foot on that faraway soil, I realized that I might already have a connection with Siberia that crossed the barriers of time and geography.

If the scientific theories of the migration of ancient Asian peoples to Turtle Island, or North America, are correct, then it is entirely possible that my ancestors either originated in what is now known as Siberia or traveled through it on their way eastward,

Journey to Altai

following the game as they moved inexorably across a strip of land now known as the Bering Land Bridge and on toward their destiny on Turtle Island.

There has been considerable debate regarding the time of those migrations over the Bering Land Bridge. The most popular theory places the earliest migration between fifteen to twenty thousand years ago; however, some scientists are cautiously suggesting that the first migrations could have occurred as early as fifty to sixty thousand years ago.

On the other hand, the original stories among the many native peoples of Turtle Island do not bother with *when*. Instead, many such stories deal with the obvious fact that we are here and that we have always been here. When a moment or an event happened so long ago that it has ceased to exist in collective memory, it then begins to exist—as my grandfather liked to say—on the other side of memory. In such an instance, *always* becomes a relative factor. And what emerges as a far more important factor is *first*.

Siberia, then, may have a direct link to my ancestry. Until my experience in Siberia I had always thought in terms of direct or family ancestry, seven or eight generations back. Beyond that, specific identities begin to fade, and one thinks of ancestry in terms of groups instead of identifiable individuals. When a name cannot be attached to a great-great-great-great-great-great-grandmother, then her identity merges with her band or tribe, such as the Turning Bear band of the Sicangu Lakota and, after that, ancestors who were Lakota. Therefore, the ancient peoples who lived in and traveled through Siberia those thousands and

Joseph Marshall III

thousands of years ago are individually and collectively nameless to me, and my connection to them can only be defined in terms of their general attributes and actions. But, they are still my ancestors and driven by need or hunger, by curiosity, or by the animosity of others, they crossed from one continent to another. They brought with them their customs, their values, their traditions, and a will and an ability to survive. Their languages may have been the basis for other languages, or they might have faded away or been absorbed into another. But the most enduring aspect of their characters and their being was their ability to adapt and survive.

It was that survival instinct which drove those ancient peoples across Siberia to stubbornly follow their destiny. I felt that to travel to that land and stand on that soil would be completing a circle—reconnecting.

From the air Moscow looked like any other major city, with its rows of huge apartment houses, its clutch of inner city high-rises, and its crisscrossing lines of streets and freeways. Then the big picture was narrowed somewhat after we landed at Sheremetyevo II International Airport and taxied to a terminal. Giant letters at the top of a building announced *MOCKBA*— Moscow. They prompted realization that I was not only literally half a world from home, but also that my knowledge of Russia was minimal and that I did not speak Russian. As the airplane rolled closer to the building and *MOCKBA* loomed larger and larger, I felt smaller and smaller and more alone than I had in years.

Clutching my briefcase after deplaning, I rolled with the tide of humanity toward stairways that led to the customs area. Customs officers sat inside glass cubicles, their eyes sweeping over documents and up over waiting faces with a routine learned many thousands of glances ago, and finally stamping their approval for people to enter or reenter the Russian Federation.

After an interminable wait, during which I struggled to be nonchalant, I finally arrived at one of the cubicles. A pair of young but tired eyes examined my papers and looked up at me for a full two seconds before handing the paper back with a nod and the hint of a smile. After another stint in a line to make a customs declaration, I was loose in Russia—with no idea how to get to Domodedevo Airport to catch the flight to Barnaul.

Those distant ancestors of mine who had eventually crossed the Bering Land Bridge did not have to contend with Moscow, I was certain. Fortunately, as I exited customs, a crowd of taxi drivers announced themselves in several languages. I did not hear Lakota, but there was a thin, strident cry among the crowd: "Taxi!"

The last time I had needed a taxi, while I was on a business trip in one of the larger cities in the United States, I had to perform several uncharacteristically acrobatic maneuvers to even facilitate a mildly curious glance from a cab driver. Outside Sheremetyevo II International Airport in Moscow, it seemed the cabbies outnumbered air travelers—unless they had seen me as the easiest mark and immediately surrounded me.

It was time to adapt and survive. As I saw it, I had two factors in my favor: first, I stood at least six inches taller than the cabbies and outweighed the largest one by at least twenty pounds, and second, I did

Joseph Marshall III

know how to say *Domodedevo*, the name of the airport I needed to reach. Without a moment's hesitation, I zeroed in on the smallest and skinniest cabbie, affected my best Will Sampson stance and stare, and growled "Domodedevo!" The little cabbie immediately drew a laminated rate card from the inside pocket of his black leather jacket, pointed to eighty dollars and said, "Forty kilometers."

Needless to say we negotiated. I pointed to twenty dollars, and he laid his finger on one hundred dollars. In the end, I paid less than eighty and more than twenty. After he dragged my large suitcase to his shiny new Mercedes and manhandled it into the trunk, we were off. After a forty-five minute ride, which basically skirted the edges of the city, we arrived at Domodedevo (domestic) Airport. The cabby seemed proud that he had gotten me there so quickly, and I, of course, could not explain to him that my flight to Barnaul did not depart for another nine hours. But he did take his money with a gracious bow and pointed to a sign that said *Intourist*.

At the Intourist desk I was given directions to the terminal from which the Barnaul flight would depart at around midnight. At midnight it was already 4 A.M. in Barnaul, and since the flight was four hours long, it would be 8 A.M. by the time I arrived. As it turned out, fog in Barnaul forced the plane to land at Novosibirsk, 150 miles northwest of Barnaul, and we passengers waited inside the terminal.

The wait at Novosibirsk was an interesting interlude—an opportunity to see a milieu of the various ethnic groups, which inhabited that part of western

Siberia. There were many brown-skinned people, some of whom were Mongolian. Many of those faces, young and old, resembled faces I had seen on just about any Indian reservation in the western United States. I could see and feel a circle closing.

Soren Ervig, who had been my seat mate on the airplane, was also there. He was a Danish author, wildlife photographer, and big game hunter who lives part of each year in Canada and speaks English better than I. He was on his way to hunt elk and spend a month in the wilds of Mongolia. Mentally converting the cash I had with me to the various local currencies, I estimated that I had more than enough to divert from Barnaul and accompany Soren to Mongolia. It would be a perfect opportunity, I reasoned, to experience yet another part of the world where my kind of people are thought to have originated. But the voice of common sense told me that my family would probably miss me, not to mention my creditors, and I did not have the proper travel papers.

Having crossed an elk hunt in Mongolia off my itinerary, I visited with Soren about our various travels. He has seen much more of the planet than I have and is steeped in interesting stories, some of which he has written about for magazine articles in the United States, Germany, Denmark, and Norway. Now and then we paused to listen to the hum of voices around us in the crowded main terminal. Although words were not understandable, facial expressions were. Nearby a small group of Khazakhstani men were jovially playing a card game atop a suitcase. In the next row of seats a young Russian couple had eyes only for each other. Behind

Joseph Marshall III

212

them a brown-skinned grandmother sat and patiently listened to the newest adventure excitedly reported by a small, energetic girl with coal black hair and shining black eyes. I had seen that look of grandmotherly love many times during my sojourn as a child, and the girl reminded me of all three of my daughters. Perhaps, I surmised, there is more to the circle.

We eventually reached Barnaul, and I said good-bye to Soren Ervig. At the terminal I was met by Gretchen Ronnow, who had by then been in Barnaul a week, and by Maria Obnarskya and Pavel Shabalin.

Barnaul was a new place, an unfamiliar environment. But Maria Obnarskya, who was small in stature with a firm handshake and precise English, could not have been nicer. Pavel Shabalin had been a pilot, a major in the air force during Russia's war with Afghanistan, flying SU-25s. Although he spoke virtually no English, in his blue eyes and in his handshake was the type of welcome that one could expect from a long-lost brother. As Maria translated introductions, I felt the mantle of being a stranger in a strange land slipping away. Somehow, even though the day of my arrival was gray and cool, Barnaul was far from being an isolated outpost of the world.

The Ob River flows northward and eventually empties into the Arctic Ocean. It flows across the West Siberian Plain, often described as the world's largest unbroken lowland. The ground in the northernmost reaches of this lowland is permanently frozen, and this permafrost is an impediment to human habitation. Hence, the southern regions have more human

Journey to Altai

habitation. It is easy to understand why one of the first trading settlements along the Ob River dates back to the early 1700s and eventually became the city of Barnaul. Not only is the climate of the region more hospitable, the Ob was then and is now a major corridor for human travel.

The phrase barnaul (barn-ah-ool), meaning "big village" or "big encampment," is rooted in one of the Altai dialects. The town was orignally a trading settlement and is now one of the few industrial cities in Siberia, with a population of 750,000 people—most of whom walk everywhere. The Barnaul State Pedagogical University, a teachers' college, is located here.

The Language Institute within the university had issued the invitations to Dr. Ronnow and me to give scholarly papers at its International Conference on Cross-Cultural Education, under the auspices of the Administration of the Altai Territory Committee of Education, directed by Vladimir Scovorodnikov. The conference itself was largely the brainchild of Dr. Edward Kuryland, Dean of the Language Institute, and a frequent visitor to Iowa.

Dr. Ronnow gave her paper the first day of the conference, and I gave mine on the second. Hers was entitled "Traveling Texts and Epistomology," which addressed the cultural aspect of foreign text interpretation in literature. Under the category of teaching culture in the classroom, mine was entitled "Positive Cross-Cultural Aspects of Teaching Foreign Language."

Most of the presenters were from Barnaul or somewhere else in Russia. Place names like Pskov, Novosibirsk, Vologda, Irkutsk, and Moscow appeared in

Joseph Marshall III

the conference program. Others listed were Alma-Ata and Ust-Kamenogorsk in Kazakhstan. And I believe at least one presenter was from Germany and another from Italy. Presenter names such as Alexandrova, Ryazanova, Sedlova, Bikkel, Akimova, and Borovikov permeated the program. Lost among them were Ronnow and Marshall.

All of these people, like Dr. Ronnow and I, had traveled to Barnaul because of a personal or professional interest in culture and education. There were no earthshaking conclusions drawn at this conference (that I know of), but perhaps something far more important than that had happened. People from different places and diverse cultural backgrounds had come together. They—we—had come together to talk, to foster awareness, and embrace diversity, rather than use it to foment suspicion or ethnocentrism. Ideas were exchanged, teaching philosophies, methods and techniques were discussed. Everything that had happened and every word spoken—in several different languages—was an affirmation and a celebration of diversity. As a Native American, it was one of the few moments in my personal and professional life when I was not forced to defend the fact that I am different. Because of that, Barnaul and the people with whom I had the closest contact will always have a special place in my heart.

I had not known what to expect from the conference. At the very least, I knew it would be a unique experience. I am not certain that my contribution to it will have any lasting impact for anyone who heard my presentation. But this conference reawakened a personal hope that it might just be possible for people to learn that diversity is common ground. On a personal level, I was honored to learn that I was probably the first Native American to visit Barnaul. And I can say beyond shadow of a doubt that Lakota was spoken for the first time ever in Barnaul in September of 1994. Hopefully, it will not be the last time.

The university had arranged for our living arrangements during our stay. In my case the Barnaul Veterans Union, an organization made up largely of veterans of the Afghanistan War, provided an apartment. One of the veterans had convinced his son Alex to move out of his apartment and turn it over to me. I was embarrassed to learn of the arrangements necessary to house me during my stay, but I also learned it was all done out of sincere generosity and warm hospitality. In addition to giving up his apartment, young Alex prepared a lavish meal for me the last night I was in Barnaul. If for whatever reason Siberia has acquired a reputation for being a cold and inhospitable place, it couldn't have been based on the people I met in Barnaul.

I had arrived in Barnaul on a Sunday about eleven in the morning. After a few hours of sleep in my apartment, I met Rustam Karshanov and Natasha Obnarskya (Maria's daughter). Both young people were students at the university and both were learning English. Rustam was studying American English and Natasha British English. They came to the apartment and while Natasha graciously cooked my first meal in Barnaul, Rustam informed me that there was to be a *banya* later in the evening.

Joseph Marshall III

Gretchen Ronnow had more or less explained the *banya* as we were riding in from the airport, with some apprehension on my behalf. But it turned out to be one of the best aspects of the entire trip, and in a sense was rather like being back on the reservation.

A *banya* is a combination of a sauna and sweatlodge, with a goodly amount of food and liquid refreshment. It is a social ritual more than a spiritual ritual, done (as far as I could gather) separately by men and women. The word *banya* is both a noun and a verb. It refers to the structure that is the sauna, the pool, and sometimes a dressing room; and it also refers to the act of having a *banya*. Loosely translated, it means "bath" or "bathroom," not to be confused with toilet.

After undressing in the outer room, the participants enter and sit on benches in the sauna as one of them pours water over the hot stones. The more water on the stones, the higher the temperature, and the temperatures can rise extremely high—sometimes so high it is difficult to breathe. During the first round, I was a second away from bolting for the door when Pavel announced it was time to go into the pool, thereby saving my dignity and reputation.

After the second round, we ate. An entire roasted chicken was put on my plate. Dessert was half a watermelon. Vodka, beer, soda pop, and water were available to wash it all down. After we ate, we did the *banya* again. In between rounds was a lot of storytelling and visiting. Since I was the newcomer from half a world away, all of the men were very curious about me and Native Americans in general.

Although the *banya* may be practiced as strictly a social ritual, one walks away from the experience feeling entirely refreshed and renewed—not unlike Native American sweatlodge ceremonies.

After our professional commitments with regard to the conference had been fulfilled, the Barnaul Veterans Union took charge of our time and itinerary, under the capable leadership of Pavel Shabilin.

First on Pavel's agenda was a boat ride up the Ob River, culminating with a meal of fish soup and a glass or two of vodka. Next, we traveled a short distance south to an area called Kalinovka for an overnight stay. Kalinovka is a beautiful forested area along the Ob. At the log house of Sergei and Oleg we were fed a sumptuous meal in preparation for some night fishing. By midnight we had established a campsite along the Ob, and for the next few hours we walked in the shallows with a large seining net. Back at the log house by 4 A.M., while the breakfast of fish soup was being prepared, I collapsed from exhaustion. The next day we returned to Barnaul, participated in the closing ceremonies of the conference, and made preparations for a long drive south into the Gorno-Altai Mountains.

It became increasingly apparent that language was the thread which was weaving the elements of this journey together. It was a barrier as well as a bond. Language was a source of frustration when it seemed that something might have been lost in the translation. The emotions, left floating in an unconnected purgatory because the essence of a thought could not be translated, cried out to be connected and given purpose. Then the thoughts which were unexpressed

Joseph Marshall III

218

soon became a burden because they became an offering never offered, leaving one with less of a connection with the person to whom they should have been conveyed. But sometimes, frustration became common ground because it helped to underscore the need to communicate.

Here I must quickly point out that the cause of any difficulty with communication was not our interpreters, Rustam Karshanov and Alexander Kuznetsev. Words are but one aspect of communicating, and with words these two young men did an admirable job. The difficulty in communicating had more to do with cultural differences that were accentuated by the differences in the languages themselves, and by differences in people themselves—just as anywhere in the world. But unlike most places in the world, our group found ways to reach one another and communicate. We kept trying because differences were not the most important aspect of our experience.

The Gorno-Altai Mountains in the southwestern portion of Siberia, north of the Chinese and Mongolian border, are among the most beautiful I have ever seen. The further we drove into them, the easier it was to imagine groups of brown-skinned people, dressed in furs and hides, walking through the mist-shrouded valleys. But it was the day we hiked up the mountain slopes that I finally understood why I had come.

We had hiked about four kilometers from our guest lodge and reached a point just beneath the highest peak in the immediate area. The air was cool, the sun was warm, the snow on the ground was crusted on its upper surface and melting underneath. And the sky was a deep, peaceful blue. Pavel had pointed out tracks in the snow. One set he said were bear, and another some type of cat. He hinted at snow leopard with a twinkle in his eye.

While the others—Rustam, Pavel, and Gretchen—rested, I sat on a promontory. In the valley to the east, a small herd of wild horses was grazing just inside the tree line, so distant that I could see them only through my binoculars; at the same time, just above me a red-tailed hawk passed so close I could see the breeze fluttering his pin feathers. But it was the mountain ranges far to the south which drew and held my attention.

To the south lay China, to the southeast was Mongolia, and the hazy, ghostly ridges I saw in the distance were the mountains of the Central Asian Range. I imagined I could see the nearly twenty-five thousand-feet-high Mount Kommunizma, near Afghanistan, although I knew it was well over a thousand miles away. What I could see framed in my field glasses were several ranges that were surely made in the same mold as the Grand Tetons back in Wyoming—bold, jagged ridges that seemed to hold up the sky itself. I put down my field glasses and took some snapshots, hoping that the camera would capture some of the drama in the distance. If not, I knew their shadowy images would stay in my heart forever.

Even though a steady breeze whistled through the pines and cedars nearby, there was a silence on the land—a silence not rooted in the absence of sound but one which emanates from the presence of harmony. I sat in the midst of a land at peace with itself, and I was

Joseph Marshall III

humbled. I had never in my life been in such a pristine and unspoiled area. And I fervently and silently prayed that the miners, loggers, and developers would never find this place.

The breezes in the pines and cedars suddenly sounded like soft, hollow voices rising and falling in a rhythm like a muted heartbeat. They were old voices, very old voices. They sounded like those I had heard rising from the tall grasses of the rolling prairie near the Little White River, back on the Rosebud Sioux Reservation, whenever the wind blew—old voices singing old songs of ancient lands.

In a way I was not surprised to find that it was difficult for me to say good-bye to the people I had met in Barnaul and to the Gorno-Altai Mountains. I made promises to my new friends, to the mountains, and to myself that I would return one day because I had made connections and reconnections. Though the people I had met were not the descendants of my distant ancestors, we still have a connection—the land itself. They live where my ancestors walked. And perhaps I did inadvertently cross an ancient trail walked by brown-skinned people so far in the past that they are on the other side of memory. And perhaps I didn't. But it does not matter, because I stood on the land and I felt their ancient spirits. They helped me to close a circle.

My memories of Barnaul and of the Gorno-Altai Mountains are of midnight fishing on the Ob River, an afternoon hike up a mountain slope, of staring at the incongruous juxtaposition of a clattering Aeroflot helicopter above a pristine, reverently quiet mountain forest, of men and women with impeccable manners, climbing in and out of cars not built for a six-foot, four-inch frame, the silvery hum of simultaneous translations in the audience as an American, a German, and an Italian offered thoughts on cross-cultural education, of dark, strong tea, tomatoes at nearly every meal, clinking vodka glasses, a walk in the mountains on a cold, starry night, hearty laughs, shy smiles, the flawless English of one Edward Kuryland, the indomitable spirit of a gentle warrior named Pavel, and the reaffirmation that to be different is the most obvious common ground there is.

After Siberia, the return trip through Moscow was merely anticlimactic. But I did walk on the cobblestones of Red Square—which is not square—and gawked up at the spires of Saint Basil's Cathedral, and caught a glimpse of the Kremlin.

From now on Barnaul, Siberia, and the Gorno-Altai Mountains will be of the utmost interest to me. With hospitality, honesty, and gentleness they softened the hard edges of the impressions and misconceptions I once had. The shadows I thought were there have diminished under the illumination of awareness; because I walked the streets, baked in a *banya*, broke bread with a brother, walked the Earth, breathed the air, touched the sky, closed a circle, and left behind a piece of my heart.

Joseph Marshall III

The Arrival of Wilderness

A pristine valley filled with pine, spruce, aspen, and birch is wedged between two mountain ranges, and a cool, silvery stream meanders through the forest, gurgling over rocks and splashing against deadfall. In the forest live birds of all sizes—from chickadees, killdeers, plovers, upland sandpipers, to red-tailed hawks, turkey vultures, and bald eagles. Mule deer, elk, moose, bears, foxes, coyotes, rabbits, beavers, shrews, squirrels, muskrats, and mice are some of the large and small four-leggeds which are also at home here. In the icy waters fed from snow melting from craggy peaks,swim brown, rainbow, and brook trout.

Several hundred miles to the southeast is another valley, a wide one filled with tall cottonwoods, oak, willow, and ash, among which crowd buffaloberry bushes and plum shrubs. This valley shares its existence with a slow, shallow river which flows through the rolling prairie grasslands. White-tailed deer and antelope come to drink from the sandy stream, in which are black bullheads and gray catfish. Badgers, raccoons, and coyotes are among the other four-leggeds which frequent this prairie habitat. In the skies above move the meadowlarks, night hawks, red-backed hawks, prairie falcons, and an occasional golden eagle.

There is one other being. There was a time when he was just another inhabitant of the valley along with the other forms of life, but no longer. Though some of his kind may well live in or near these valleys, he is separated from them by his dwelling and his lifestyle. But he is disconnected even more by how he defines them and all other parts of the natural world. Man has become merely a visitor in these valleys and now calls them *wilderness*.

Wilderness—be it glacier, swamp, mountain range, prairie grassland, boreal forest, desert, marsh, or seashore—in most dictionaries is defined as "an uncultivated and unihabited region." The semantics of wilderness is obviously influenced by man's estimation of man's importance. If man has not plowed and sowed seeds in it and/or does not live there (never mind other species), then it is wilderness. Anthropocentric arrogance prompts man to define something based on his absence or disassociation from it, implying that there can be no other way to define the natural environment.

Such self-aggrandizement has long ago resulted in man separating himself from the total (planetary) environment and the birth of concepts such as "man and nature," "man against nature," "the cruelty of nature," "the natural environment," "wild animals," and "wilderness." Such defining concepts show that man has not only separated himself from the environment, he has placed himself in opposition to it, given himself equal or greater status, and has created artificial domains. These are the reasons why man looks at the many facets of the natural environment and sees water, timber, minerals, animals, and land as "resources" for his use and disposal. This perception is arrogantly summed up on a bumper sticker that states *Wilderness: Land of No Use.* But such concepts did not always prevail on this continent.

Someone once said that "the great arrogance of the present is to forget the intelligence of the past." Such an observation rings true with regard to many, many facets of human history, but it seems to be an especially sad reality when it comes to mankind's self-imposed exile from the total environment.

Technology has given modern man the ability to impact his environment like no other generation has. That kind of ability seems to have totally obliterated a basic truth: that at a point in the evolution of every human society, usually at that level characterized as "tribal," there was a philosophy of functioning and existing within the parameters of the total environment, as opposed to one of human dominance or control.

Although Native Americans by and large no longer function at a *primitive* tribal level, we are on the average only four or five generations removed from a time when we did. Whether we were whalers on the Northwest coast, built longhouses in the Northeast forests, chased buffalo on the Plains, lived in adobe houses atop desert plateaus, or paddled through the water ways of a swamp, we lived in daily direct contact with the environment. That was the reality of

Joseph Marshall III

226

existence for us, no matter the specific region, terrain, or climate we called home.

Our very survival depended on intimate knowledge of the land and all of its other inhabitants. We knew where the most productive chokecherry bushes grew year after year, for example, and which were likely to bear some fruit even in the dry years. We knew which routes the caribou were likely to take during spring and autumn migrations and positioned hunters accordingly. And we knew that when the deer browsed more than usual, or their winter hair appeared earlier in the season than was customary, that a hard winter was probably coming. While such knowledge was essential to survival and comfort, it also provided a broad and extensive awareness of all other forms of life with which we had regular contact as well as knowledge of relationships with one another. The one inevitable conclusion, the one unavoidable fact was that all species, including humans, were part of the same, total environment. This reality is reflected in many of the human languages of Turtle Island (North America).

In my native language of Lakota, for example, there is no word for *wilderness*. There is a word for *wild*, which is *watogla*, but it has nothing to do with wilderness. It means "untamed" or "behaving in an unmannerly fashion." Neither meaning is associated with the natural environment (from time to time they do apply to my brothers-in-law, however).

Before intense contact with Europeans and Euro-Americans, the word *manitu* came closest to their concept of wilderness. It meant "away or apart from the village or encampment." When it became

The Arrival of Wilderness

necessary to conceptualize and then find a word to label the Euro-American idea of "wilderness," *manitu* was the logical choice. It is important to remember, however, that in the mind of the pre-European Lakota speaker *manitu* simply meant a different place and not a different concept of a place dependent on his presence or absence.

As further illustration, consider how a contemporary Lakota speaker would translate *wolf* and explain its meaning. *Sunkmanitu tanka* is our equivalent for wolf, and its contemporary literal meaning is "big dog of the wild" (or *wilderness*). The pre-European and more traditional translation is apparently "great" or "greater dog who lives away from the encampment"; there is, of course, *sunkmanitu*, which is the word for "coyote." Then there is *mayaca*, which is an even older word for "wolf"; the decline of its use may indicate that the usage of *sunkamanitu tanka* may well have resulted from a Euro-American effort to describe some aspect of the wolf's character or behavior in order to facilitate a Lakota translation. There are also other Lakota words for "coyote," such as *masleca*, which seems to add to the logic of the previous suggestion. Furthermore, none of the older Lakota words for "coyote" or "wolf" have semantic links to the notion of "wilderness," which substantiates the argument that it was not an operative concept.

Another affirmation of a Lakota attitude with regard to other forms of life is subtly reflected in references such as *hehaka oyate, mato oyate,* and *zintkala oyate,* meaning "elk people," "bear people," and "bird people" respectively. These were not animal names

Joseph Marshall III

228

used as labels for people, but rather the word *oyate,* which means "people," "nation," "band," or "tribe" ascribed to those species (and others as well). This association indicates an awareness that other species that shared the environment had their own societies with structure, behavior, and lifestyle peculiar to each. Such concepts did not derive from man paternalistically anthropomorphizing animals; they were the result of man recognizing the viability, vitality, and uniqueness that was common to all species, including himself. This was, after all, how things were—reality.

Throughout Turtle Island there were many different cultural views of mankind's place in the world, but all were rooted in the reality of existence within the total environment. To put it another way, the pre-European inhabitants of Turtle Island realized how things were relative to all aspects of their environment and accepted the situation. Furthermore, acceptance of the reality of physical existence was not a matter of humans *lowering* themselves; it simply meant realizing that humans had a *place* and a *purpose* like every other form of life. Neither did it mean a romantic, utopian lifestyle requiring demonstrations of "brotherly" love with a quota of trees to hug. But it did mean being part of the reality.

One of my great-grandfathers is buried in an unmarked grave on a grassy hillside just above a river. No one is certain of the exact location, but some summers there is one area where the grass is thicker and greener. That great-grandfather was a healer. Some would be more familiar with the term medicine man. He died young, at the age of forty-nine, in 1911. My grandmother said that he offered too many times to take upon himself the pain and discomfort of his patients. She also told me that her father was buried without a casket, according to his wishes. He told his family that nothing should prevent his return to the Earth.

There is no more powerful example of the understanding of the reality of life, of the existence we share on this Earth with many other species. The explicit instructions for his own burial are indicative of the fact that my great-grandfather did not consider himself above or apart from all that was life and the reality of existence. What, then, is the difference between a people who understand the reality of existence and a people who do not? I believe it is arrogance.

Arrogance is defined as "exaggerating one's own importance." With that in mind, consider the following scenario.

Picture an ancient bison hunt on the northern Plains of Turtle Island. All of the able-bodied males from the community or village have managed to maneuver and then chase a large herd toward a precipice, and hundreds are driven over the edge. Even before the dust has settled, the human hunters begin to butcher the carcasses and eventually take only thirty or forty of the bison and leave the rest. Our arrogance as humans might lead us to judge that those ancient hunters were guilty of monumental waste. But what about the coyotes, bears, wolves, buzzards, magpies, and innumerable others who eventually took their share of the kill? And what about the Earth itself, which is still in the process of reclaiming what is left of the bison? To judge this hunt as a waste of resources because humans

Joseph Marshall III

did not consume or use all of the bison killed would be
the epitome of anthropocentric arrogance.

As a boy of seven I saw how arrogance is an
operative factor. My grandparents had land on what was
still then the northern part of the Rosebud Sioux
Indian Reservation, in south-central South Dakota.
Early that summer my grandfather decided to repair a
portion of the fence around the quarter section (160
acres) on which we lived to prevent cattle from an
adjacent ranch from wandering into our pasture. The
repair work consisted of tightening and restapling
strands of barbed wire. On a particular slope the strands
of wire had been overgrown by some thick shrubs,
inside of which was a meadowlark's nest complete with
eggs. Because retightening the bottom strand of wire
in that particular spot would have meant disturbing the
nest and the eggs, my grandfather rerouted the fence
just enough to go around the shrubs.

The following year a neighboring rancher
leased our land to pasture cattle and decided that a
portion of the fence we had repaired the previous year
had to be replaced. So he came with his post hole
digger and a scraper mounted on the back of a tractor.
With the scraper he literally obliterated anything that
was in the way of the fence line, including the shrubs,
which sheltered yet another nest full of meadowlark
eggs. Since that day I have hated fences.

Several years ago I listened to and watched a
television news story about a small amount of nuclear
waste that had been dumped in a swampy area in the
southeastern part of the United States. The half-life of
that waste, it was reported, is twenty-four thousand years.

Therefore, that acre or two of swamp will be devoid of life for millenniums.

But if the building of that fence and the clandestine disposal of nuclear waste are testaments to human arrogance and disregard for the environment, there are equally compelling lessons from the ancient and recent past of Turtle Island which illustrate the opposite viewpoint.

It is probably a little-known fact that many of the nomadic pre-European hunting tribes of Turtle Island emulated the wolf. The wolf as a hunter has few equals. He certainly has impressive physical attributes: size, speed, strength, powerful jaws, keen sense of smell, sharp eyesight, and outstanding hearing. Man obviously did not possess those attributes and never would. But there was a characteristic of the wolf he could emulate—perseverence. When the wolf hunts, he fails more often than he succeeds, but he does not quit. Therefore, man decided that he must also learn perseverence.

However, the wolf was more than the epitome of hunter for early man on Turtle Island. Some people of Turtle Island observed that family was important to the wolf and that wolves were aggressively protective and extremely indulgent parents. Furthermore, man saw that the wolf protected den and territory against any and all enemies, regardless of number or size; these were virtues and characteristics of great value that man could emulate. It is important to note that not all of the people of Turtle Island saw a need to emulate the wolf, but most, at least, did not fear or despise him.

When the European came to Turtle Island, he brought with him his fear of the wolf. It is difficult to

Joseph Marshall III

ascertain precisely when European man began to fear the wolf, but I suspect that it was a consequence of the judgment of an entire species based on the actual or perceived behavior of one of its members. There are a few wolves left in some of the northern European countries. During a recent trip I was surprised to learn that there are still occasional reports of wolves attacking humans; but the "attacks" always occurred during hunting season, and the "attacking" wolves seemed to inevitably single out hunters armed with rifles. There are no reports of wolves attacking unarmed hikers or campers.

Today, arrogance has not only enabled humans to place themselves apart from and above other species and redefine the environment from which they have separated themselves, arrogance has also become the basis for claiming the right to destroy other species with impunity. Our arrogance outweighs enlightenment to the point that we still cave in to ancient and misbegotten fears about certain species such as the wolf. And if we can so easily lose touch with reality in regard to one aspect of the natural environment, could we do the same in regard to the total environment?

It does appear that we humans may have defined ourselves out of any direct relationship or responsibility to what we now term the "natural environment." We have created isolated, artificial environments for ourselves that we control with the touch of a button or the flick of a switch. But we seem to have also isolated ourselves from a basic, ancient reality as well—the cause and effect interrelationship. That is, we seem to have forgotten that whatever happens to the natural environment will affect us: conversely, what we think and do will have an effect on the natural environment. In that reality lies a part of, if not the entire, solution.

Consider that we have all come to a valley, any of the valleys described earlier. Consider that we must cross that valley in order to complete our journey. The thoughts and emotions we take with us into that valley will correspond to our awareness of its realities; our experiences in the valley will reflect our knowledge of it. Consider the following two scenerios.

On the one hand we might be afraid to cross the valley because we know little or nothing about the inhabitants of the valley. Their appearance, movements, and voices would be new and strange. We might not be able to distinguish the warning "woof" of a wary white-tailed buck from the inquiring, curious "woof" of a male grizzly. And if it is autumn and there is a loud and persistent buzzing in the forest, would we know that it comes from an insect no larger than half the size of a thumb—the locust? Or would we think it is something ready to pounce or strike? More than likely we would consider the forest as a mass of tree trunks and a tangle of branches, since we might not know that there are several different types of trees with different characteristics and separate niches in the ecology of the valley. Or that the circle of flattened grass is the daytime bed of a nocturnal deer, rather than a giant footprint of a who-knows-what. The greater the ignorance, the greater the fear.

On the other hand, we might walk into that valley unafraid because of an awareness of its terrain and ecology. We might not know this particular valley intimately, but we can approach it with the sense that we have been in places like it before. We might pause at that circle of matted grass and know that a white-tailed buck was disturbed by our approach and left his bed, stopping some distance away to "woof" his indignation and warn others that we are here. We might hear the buzz of the seventeen-year locust and marvel at the coincidence which brought us here at the moment of his emergence from a seventeen-year hibernation. We might look at the trees and search the forest floor for acorns from the oak and bristly cones from the giant pine. We might seek the shadowy folds of the forest in order to sit in the cool shade, to take the time to observe and appreciate our surroundings rather than hurry through the valley.

Depending on our level of knowledge and awareness, once on the other side of the valley we would pause to look back—and either breathe a sigh of relief for having emerged unscathed or voice a reluctant good-bye. We have either walked through the valley or we have escaped the wilderness.

It is a fact that the concept of wilderness has crept into the Lakota language and has changed the meaning of *manitu* from "away from the encampment" to "wilderness."

It is a fact that the current reality of our existence segregates, if not exiles, man from a portion of it. Wilderness has arrived, and we look at it in terms of resources to be identified, harvested, used and—too often abused—and disposed of in the end. Wilderness is minerals, water, timber, hunting, recreation, undeveloped land, jobs, and maybe a vacation or a retirement hideaway. We speak grandiosely in terms of "managing" those "resources"—not necessarily for the sake of the water, trees, and land, but for our use and consumption. That is the current reality. That should not mean, however, that it has to be the only reality or that the intelligence of the past should be cast aside.

My grandparents taught me many lessons, not so much by the instructions they gave but by how they lived. Both of my maternal grandparents loved the outdoor away-from-the-house environment. For reasons that are now vague in my mind, they disdained ownership of automobiles, preferring instead to travel by horse-drawn wagon. I will never forget the forays to dig wild turnips, pick chokecherries, knock down buffaloberries, to gather and pile dry wood for winter fuel, hand carry buckets of water from a spring during every season of the year—and much, much more. But there was one simple act which was, to me, a profound gesture of acknowledgment. Both of them liked to sit on the ground, remove their shoes, and caress the Earth with their hands and bare feet. As a boy I did it because they did it. Now I do it every so often because I finally understand why they did it. To touch the Earth and to accept its silence is to be calmed by its strength, to be centered, and to feel the sacredness of all life. It is to know that one is a part of a whole, a total environment that is defined by all of its components and not by the absence of one.

Joseph Marshall III

THE RED CRANE LITERATURE SERIES

Dancing to Pay the Light Bill:
Essays on New Mexico and the Southwest
by Jim Sagel

Death in the Rain
a novel by Ruth Almog

The Death of Bernadette Lefthand
a novel by Ron Querry

New Mexico Poetry Renaissance
edited by Sharon Niederman and Miriam Sagan

Stay Awhile: A New Mexico Sojourn
essays by Toby Smith

Spinning Sun, Grinning Moon
novellas by Max Evans

This Dancing Ground of Sky:
The Selected Poetry of Peggy Pond Church
by Peggy Pond Church

Winter of the Holy Iron
a novel by Joseph Marshall III

Working in the Dark: Reflections of a Poet of the Barrio
writings by Jimmy Santiago Baca